Northamptonshire Steam

MICHAEL WELCH

FEATURING COLOUR PHOTOGRAPHY BY TOMMY TOMALIN

Published by Rails Publishing

Printed by Parksons Graphics

© Michael Welch 2016
Layout by Michael Welch. Typesetting
and book production by Lucy Frontani.

Front Cover: Photographed on a beautiful
spring evening, BR Standard Class 9F
No.92070, hauling a northbound empty
mineral working, passes Merry Tom crossing,
just under a mile north of Pitsford &
Brampton station, on 9th May 1962. The
photographer recorded the time of the
photograph as 7.00pm which suggests he
had decided to go out after work to take
advantage of the perfect weather conditions
– what a brilliant idea! *Tommy Tomalin*

Back Cover: The 9.46am Peterborough
(East) to Northampton (Castle) train rolls
into Wellingborough (London Road) behind
Stanier Class 5MT 4-6-0 No.44682 on
11th April 1964; two lonely prospective
passengers wait on the otherwise
deserted platform. The junction signal
in the distance indicates where the spur
line to Wellingborough (Midland Road)
station diverged from the 'main' line to
Peterborough. *Edwin Wilmshurst*

Title Page: The 12.28pm 'all stations' train
from Northampton to Peterborough pauses at
Northampton Bridge Street station to pick up
passengers on 14th April 1962. This cross-
country jaunt generally occupied 1½ hours
and, unfortunately, the sparse service of six
weekday trains in the early 1960s proved
that few people wished to travel between
those places. The motive power for this
train, Thompson-designed B1 Class 4-6-0
No.61095, is especially interesting because
it was fitted with a self weighing tender.
Ron Gammage

Details of Michael Welch's other
railway titles can be found at
www.capitaltransport.com

Introduction

I have made many journeys through Northamptonshire over the years, usually travelling at reasonable speed along the West Coast Main Line (WCML) to and from destinations in the north of England or Scotland. I had no idea where the county's borders were located but at least had a brief glimpse of Northampton station on one occasion when going home on a diverted WCML train, my thoughts, however, were probably focussed on the extra time the journey would take and the expected arrival time in London. I almost certainly gave no thought to the fascinating network of routes that criss-crossed the county, or their history.

This is a pity because, amazingly, due to the county's geographical position straddling a large tract of central England, main lines of five of the pre-nationalisation companies passed through it and, moreover, there was a number of secondary and branch lines, largely fanning out from Northampton. The Great Western Railway's (GWR) Oxford to Banbury route ran just inside the Northamptonshire border for a few miles between Aynho and Banbury while the London & North Eastern Railway (LNER) operated lines around Peterborough, but their principal route, the East Coast Main Line (ECML), ran within the county in splendid isolation for a short distance whilst not connecting directly with any other lines. No suitable photographs of trains on the ECML were received for publication in this album and it was therefore decided to omit the route from the book. In between the GWR and LNER lines, the London Midland & Scottish Railway (LMSR) almost had a monopoly, the principal exception being the Great Central (GC) route which, due to its origins, came under the jurisdiction of the LNER.

The oldest of the main line trunk routes was (what later became) the West Coast Main Line which was opened between Euston and Birmingham on 17th September 1838, but this unfortunately by-passed Northampton due to its position in the Nene valley. Robert Stephenson, the route's principal engineer, was concerned that the relatively steep gradients required might be beyond the capabilities of the steam locomotives then available. He liked 'to select a line on which the difference between the highest and lowest levels is the best which the character of the country will admit of'. In addition to those problems there was opposition from the townspeople for a time, and the local landed gentry who feared the railway would do considerable damage to their estates. Northampton was not rail connected until the branch from Blisworth was brought into use on 13th May 1845. In the late 1870s the quadrupling of the WCML resulted in the construction of the Northampton loop which opened on 3rd April 1882. While the WCML served few major population centres in the county the reverse is true of the Midland Railway's (MR) main line which was extended from Leicester to Bedford on 8th May 1857 and passed through Desborough, Kettering and Wellingborough; the (then) village of Corby was added to the system in 1880. Prior to the opening of the MR's own line to London heavy coal traffic was routed along the old Midland Counties Railway line from Leicester to Rugby.

The sad tale of the GC line is well known and its rise and fall in the relatively short space of 70 years has been well documented. An offshoot of the Manchester, Sheffield & Lincolnshire Railway, the 'London Extension', which carried its first public passenger trains on 15th March 1899, managed to avoid all major settlements in Northamptonshire, traversing miles of empty countryside between Rugby and Aylesbury, though it has to be said that this undulating, rural part of the county undoubtedly had its attractions. The GC line fell victim to BR's desire to rid itself of (what were perceived to be) 'duplicate routes' and inter-regional rivalries are also thought to have influenced the decision to close the line. The GC route was deliberately and systematically stripped of traffic over a number of years, beginning with the Marylebone to Manchester through trains which were withdrawn in 1960. Three years later local services between Aylesbury and Rugby were axed, together with the entire Sunday service north of Aylesbury. The line's heavy freight traffic was diverted to other routes in 1965 leaving an increasingly unreliable, mostly steam-hauled service of three Marylebone to Nottingham semi-fast trains, and their corresponding return workings, to cater for what little traffic remained. The line was largely closed in September 1966, thus ending its protracted agony.

Northamptonshire certainly had its share of lines with little traffic potential, proposed by promoters with apparently unlimited optimism. The ill-fated Northampton & Banbury Railway, authorised in 1863, never reached either town on its own tracks while another fanciful scheme was the East & West Junction Railway from Towcester to Stratford-upon-Avon which was authorised in 1864. This company later extended eastwards to Olney, and westwards to Broom, but later these lines were amalgamated to form part of the Stratford-upon-Avon & Midland Junction Railway. The very meagre passenger service between Blisworth and Stratford was an early casualty, being withdrawn as long ago as 5th April 1952, but sections of the route were useful for cross country freight working and survived much longer.

Northamptonshire could hardly claim to have any spectacular routes but this was compensated to some degree by the particularly interesting motive power that could be seen in the county. In 1927 the LMSR introduced the first of its Beyer Garratt locomotives, an unmistakable design of effectively two engines in one employing a single large boiler; the design was patented by the Beyer Peacock Company in Manchester. The majority of these locomotives were equipped with conical coal bunkers that could be revolved or oscillated by a small two-cylinder steam engine. Unfortunately, the class was not entirely successful and throughout its life was plagued by wheel bearing problems. While the majority of the locomotives were stationed at Toton, near Nottingham, some were based at Wellingborough and all could be seen plodding along the Midland main line on heavy coal trains to keep the fires burning in the capital. The 'Garratts' were replaced in the mid-1950s by newly built BR Standard Class 9F 2-10-0s but ten of these machines, Nos.92020 to 92029, were definitely very far from being 'standard'. They were experimentally equipped with Crosti boilers, of a type that had been pioneered in Italy, these being designed to reduce coal consumption. The most distinctive feature of these locomotives was the exhaust outlet beside the boiler in front of the cab, the chimney being used solely for lighting up purposes; all of the locomotives were shedded at Wellingborough. Like their 'Garratt' predecessors, the Crosti locomotives were not an unqualified success, in this case due to excessive corrosion in the smokebox and pre-heater, and all spent considerable periods in the late 1950s dumped out of use prior to rebuilding to conventional operation.

Compilation of this album would not have been possible without the assistance of the many photographers who submitted pictures and thanks are offered to those gentlemen; perhaps it is appropriate to offer special thanks to Tommy Tomalin for his outstanding contribution. Pictures from the R C Riley collection were kindly made available by Rodney Lissenden. In addition, Bob Dalton, Chris Evans, Dave Fakes, John Langford, Graham Onley and Terry Phillips read the proof and suggested many worthwhile corrections and improvements to the text.

Michael Welch
Burgess Hill
West Sussex

Contents

Map of railway routes in Northamptonshire
(including parts of surrounding counties)

The railway system in Northamptonshire
changed considerably during the years covered
by this book so it is not possible to provide a
map that would be valid for the entire period.

The Manchester Sheffield & Lincolnshire Railway (MSLR), formed in 1847 by the amalgamation of three other railways, was for some time led by Sir Edward Watkin, an enterprising and dynamic chairman who was determined to expand the company's system. On 28th March 1893 the MSLR obtained an Act of Parliament to build a line from Annesley, Nottinghamshire, to Quainton, Buckinghamshire, where it made a connection with the Metropolitan Railway. A new terminus was constructed in London at Marylebone. The new route, which was built to the Berne loading gauge, opened on 15th March 1899 and was characterised by a moderate ruling gradient of 1 in 176, the use of distinctive blue brick for many civil engineering works and, remarkably, a total lack of any level crossings. The status of the MSLR was transformed from that of a provincial cross-country railway to a major trunk route and the company changed its name to 'Great Central' (GC). The new line undoubtedly had an atmosphere all of its own but suffered considerable disadvantages because nearly all of the major population centres it served had alternative routes to London and, furthermore, the Great Central had a 45 miles-long stretch between Rugby and Aylesbury where it passed through a very thinly populated part of middle England and made few connections with other routes. Residents of Harrow and Aylesbury, however, would probably have regarded the line as an indispensible link to the Midlands and north of England! On 1st February 1958 the operation of the GC line was transferred from the Eastern Region to the London Midland Region and from that date the writing was clearly on the wall for the line which was seen as an expensive duplicate route but, in reality, inter-regional rivalries also played a part. The first blow was struck in January 1960 when through expresses from Manchester (London Road)/Sheffield (Victoria) to Marylebone were withdrawn. Local passenger services were withdrawn between Aylesbury and Sheffield on 4th March 1963, with the exception of a few trains between Rugby and Nottingham which were retained for the benefit of workpeople. Sunday trains, which had been some of the best patronised on the route, were withdrawn from 10th March. This left three weekday semi-fast trains between Marylebone and Nottingham and return, a Bournemouth to York and *vice versa* cross country service and a variety of overnight trains and holiday extras which did not contribute materially to the service. There was still a high proportion of steam working but many of the locomotives used on the passenger services were in a parlous condition and failures in traffic were all too frequent. The future of the line clearly hinged on the continuation of very heavy goods traffic but the withdrawal of the Hull to Swindon fish trains in February 1965 was an ominous sign and through goods services ceased from 14th June 1965; all summer Saturday passenger workings were diverted to other routes. Here the 5.15pm Nottingham (Victoria) to Marylebone train, hauled by indescribably filthy Stanier Class 5MT No.45426, has just crossed the county border into Buckinghamshire on 23rd June 1966, just over two months before the line closed from 5th September. The 22-arch, 320 feet-long Brackley viaduct, which crosses the river Ouse marking the border with Northamptonshire, can be seen in the distance. *Tommy Tomalin*

2nd ORDINARY RETURN   ORDINARY RETURN 2nd

Brackley (Central)   Helmdon (Sulgrave)
HELMDON (Sulgrave)   to BRACKLEY (Central)
(M) Fare 2/6   Fare 2/6 (M)
For conditions see over   For conditions see over

Above left Brackley, a relatively small market town close to the border of both Oxfordshire and Buckinghamshire, was served by two stations, 'Central' on the GC line, and 'Town' on the Verney Junction to Banbury Merton Street line which closed to passengers north of Buckingham on 2nd January 1961. Originally, it had been planned to construct the entrance to Brackley Central on a bridge just north of the station that carried a main road but wiser counsels prevailed and a lay-by was built on the west side of the line which provided access to the main entrance. The line's promoters envisaged building a link to Northampton at one stage and the station was laid out with sufficient space to facilitate this, but nothing came of the idea. The station's busiest periods were probably the beginning and end of school terms, there being a number of boarding schools in the area. However, the local passengers must have keenly felt the loss of their line because, unlike most points served by the GC route, there was no alternative station in the town leaving travellers with the choice of using Banbury or Bletchley stations, both of which were some distance away. This picture shows a scene that was commonplace during the last months of the line's existence as Stanier Class 5MT No.45267 takes water while working the 5.15pm Nottingham Victoria to Marylebone on 15th August 1966. The GC line was by this date the only northbound route out of London with regular steam haulage and was well patronised by steam buffs. *Robin Patrick*

Left The small and compact island platform wayside stations favoured by the GC are exemplified here by this picture of Helmdon station taken on 2nd March 1963. Note the tiny booking office window and huge station nameboard. This shot was taken towards the end of a spell of intensely cold winter weather to which the partially snow-covered field in the background bears ample testament. The stationmaster's house is visible on the left of the photograph. The village of Helmdon was adjacent to the station but Sulgrave was three miles distant. The station was kitted out with a fine collection of posters, no doubt inviting passengers to visit other parts of the country by train, but it was too late for any prospective travellers because the station was closed two days later when local services on the GC line, apart from those between Rugby and Nottingham, were withdrawn. *Tommy Tomalin*

Above The Culworth Junction to Banbury line, opened in 1900, was a vital link to GWR territory and the south and west of England and latterly came to be regarded as the 'main line' while the route to Marylebone was seen as a long branch from Woodford Halse which was then known as 'Woodford & Hinton'. In this portrait the Banbury line is seen diverging to the right while the route to the Capital goes more or less straight ahead. The junction was located about two miles south-east of Woodford and must have been a really lonely spot for the signalman, particularly on night duty. Here, the 4.38pm Marylebone to Nottingham (Victoria) train, with Stanier Class 5MT 4-6-0 No.44847 in charge, is seen passing Culworth Junction signal box on 17th August 1966. *Tommy Tomalin*

In the closing years of BR steam traction little attempt was made to keep locomotives clean, except for some prestigious express passenger locomotives, and most were in deplorable condition. An exception, however, is Stanier Class 8F 2-8-0 No.48121 which is depicted passing beneath the handsome Eydon Road bridge, just south of Woodford Halse station, on 12th October 1963; presumably No.48121 had recently been repainted during a main works overhaul. The train had just passed the junction with a very tightly curved spur to the former Stratford-upon-Avon & Midland Junction (SMJR) line which crossed over the GC line immediately south of the photographer's viewpoint. The SMJR line diverged at Woodford No.4 signal box which can just be identified through the left-hand arch of the bridge. *Neville Simms*

2nd-SINGLE SINGLE-2nd

Charwelton to

Charwelton
Woodford Halse

Charwelton
Woodford Halse

WOODFORD HALSE

(M)   0/6   Fare   0/6   (M)

For conditions see over   For conditions see over

7339   7339

Photographed from the bridge seen in the previous picture, an enormously long goods train with another 8F Class, No.48027, in charge heads southwards from Woodford Halse on 18th April 1964. A goods working can also be seen on the down line, just about to pass through the station. This photograph provides a closer view of the spur line to Woodford West Junction on the SMJR route which goes off to the left. Passenger services on the cross country SMJR Blisworth to Stratford-upon-Avon route were an early closure casualty, being withdrawn from 7th April 1952 while the final regular passenger trains on the spur from Woodford West junction to Woodford & Hinton (as it was then known) were withdrawn even earlier, from 31st May 1948. *Neville Simms*

Woodford Halse station was constructed on the standard GC island platform principle and in this picture the 4.38pm Marylebone to Nottingham (Victoria) train, headed by Class 5MT 4-6-0 No.44941, is seen awaiting departure on 14th May 1966. The station was known for many years as 'Woodford & Hinton', the name being changed in 1948. The platform on the right, built to handle the local trains to Banbury, was originally constructed of wood but was replaced in 1956 by a more substantial concrete version. It was always referred to as the 'wooden platform' a description that survived to the end despite its reconstruction in concrete! The arrival of the railway at Woodford Halse transformed a quiet Northamptonshire village to a busy community and the coming of the railway attracted many newcomers; it is recorded that the population doubled, reaching a peak of 1,700 in the early 1930s. Needless to say, a large proportion of the villagers worked on the railway in some capacity. Woodford's strategic location adjacent to the SMJR and important link to Banbury made it an important cross-country railway centre, especially for goods traffic, and extensive goods sidings were laid. Movements at Woodford Halse were controlled by no fewer than four signal boxes. During the Second World War increasing goods traffic prompted the laying of more sidings north of the engine shed in an attempt to cope with the demands of war time.
Edwin Wilmshurst

The run-down of the GC route was undertaken in stages over a period of six years, one of the most significant dates being 3rd March 1963 when Sunday services operated for the last time. The summer 1959 timetable advertised four Sunday daytime trains in each direction between Marylebone and Sheffield (Victoria) some of which continued to Manchester (London Road). In addition, there were a few intermediate services plus one or two short workings between London and Brackley or Woodford Halse, including one second class only train that left Marylebone for Brackley at the ungodly hour of 5.30am on a Sunday morning! So, there was considerable activity on the GC line even on a Sunday, but this came to an abrupt halt from 10th March 1963 when the Sunday trains were withdrawn and the line closed between Sheffield and Aylesbury on that day. In this picture the 10.10am Nottingham (Victoria) to Marylebone train, with 'Black Five' No.45285 in charge, is seen accelerating away from Woodford Halse on 3rd March. The winter of 1962/63 had been particularly harsh and the last vestiges of the snows can be seen in the field on the right of the shot.
Tommy Tomalin

Woodford Halse shed, located on the east side of the line north of the station, was a six-road affair and its huge coaling plant, which dated from 1935, was a landmark for many miles around. There was a carriage and wagon repair shop adjacent to the shed so the depot and its immediate environs were clearly a hive of round-the-clock activity. The shed roof was renewed, including new ventilators, in 1959 so the depot was presumably thought to have a secure future at that time. In the early years of the BR regime Woodford shed's allocation was almost entirely made up of former London & North Eastern Railway classes including a large complement of former GCR 2-8-0s, B1 Class 4-6-0s and K3 Class 2-6-0s, though it should be noted that the first-mentioned were soon replaced by WD Class

2-8-0s. Following the transfer of the GC route to the LMR in 1958 former LMSR classes started to be drafted to the line, one of the most startling developments being the allocation of 'Royal Scot' Class 4-6-0s to Annesley shed in late 1962. Woodford Halse shed's complement of WD Class locomotives was gradually replaced by 8F Class 2-8-0s during 1963 and by the summer only two WDs were still working from the shed. Despite the changing scene former LNER classes could still be observed, particularly V2 Class 2-6-2s on goods workings from York, and there must have been some excitement on 19th March 1962 when Gresley A3 Pacific No.60078 *Night Hawk* worked through to Banbury and later returned with the 7.30pm Swindon to York passenger train. Woodford shed was closed from 14th June 1965 and most of its locomotives departed on Friday 11th June running either to Bletchley via the Calvert spur or to Annesley; it is recorded that the last engines to leave the shed were Class 8Fs Nos. 48005/61/121 which left for Bletchley during the afternoon of 12th June. Eight locomotive crews were still based at Woodford for London services, booking on and off at the station – what a comedown. Here, BR Standard Class 5MT 4-6-0 No.73000 poses at Woodford shed on 25th February 1964. *Graham Onley*

The LMR was frequently accused of moving locomotives due for withdrawal to the GC line and certainly the disgraceful external condition of 'Royal Scot' Class 4-6-0 No.46165 *The Ranger (12th London Regt.)* does little to inspire confidence; it was photographed at Woodford Halse shed on 8th August 1964. In mid-1964 it was one of five locomotives of this class, out of a total of 16 survivors, based at Annesley for GC line passenger work; it was withdrawn in November 1964. *Rodney Lissenden*

The GC line was gradually stripped of traffic over a period of some years and died a lingering death. Woodford Halse had in many respects been the nerve centre of the southern end of the route with a connection to the SMJR, fair sized motive power depot and extensive marshalling yards but by mid-1966 very little remained apart from the main line tracks, station plus a few sidings and much of the huge site had become a wasteland. Everywhere dereliction and decay stared one in the face, a very depressing situation for dedicated local railwaymen who had given the best years of their lives to the line. To all intents and purposes the GC's fate was sealed when the substantial through goods traffic was re-routed away from the line in June 1965, but it had to drag itself on for a further 15 months until the inevitable closure between Rugby and Aylesbury finally came. Here the 5.15pm Nottingham (Victoria) to Marylebone train, hauled by filthy Stanier Class 5MT No.44835, passes the site of the former shed on 25th May 1966 with the coaling tower still standing defiantly on the right of the shot. During the following week demolition of the shed complex commenced but the stores building and concrete coaling plant remained *in situ* for some time afterwards. On 25th February 1968 Royal Marines explosive experts were called in to demolish the last two structures and this event received full coverage in both the national and local media. Blast off was timed for 8.30am and the 'coaler' did not offer much resistance, but the sturdily-built Edwardian stores complex apparently needed five separate charges of plastic explosive before it succumbed. *Tommy Tomalin*

The closing years of the GC were not all doom and gloom however – well, not quite. On 25th May 1963 Leicester City played Manchester United in the FA Cup Final at Wembley and in view of the GC line's close proximity to Wembley stadium a series of special trains for Leicester supporters was routed along the GC line. Some of the football specials left the east Midlands city quite early and this provided a golden opportunity for lineside photographers because, not only was the early morning light at its best, they had the added bonus of locomotives that had been specially cleaned for the occasion and looked really immaculate in the sunshine. In this picture Stanier Class 6P5F 'Jubilee' 4-6-0 No.45626 *Seychelles* takes the 8.46am Leicester Central to Marylebone train southwards over Charwelton troughs at 9.35am. *Tommy Tomalin*

The icy wastes of Northamptonshire. A Marylebone to Nottingham working, headed by 'Royal Scot' Class 7P 4-6-0 No.46142 *The York & Lancaster Regiment*, approaches Charwelton station on 16th February 1963. The train had just passed over Charwelton water troughs but if the crew wanted to replenish No.46142's water supplies they would have been out of luck on this occasion, the troughs being completely frozen over due to the sub zero temperatures that Great Britain was experiencing at the time. Like so many locomotives working on the GC route at that time No.46142 is in deplorable condition but was destined to soldier on for almost a further year. *Neville Simms*

A snowy landscape. The winter of 1962/63 was, as previously mentioned, notable for a prolonged spell of bitterly cold weather which is exemplified here by this portrait of V2 Class 2-6-2 No.60967 steaming southwards through Charwelton on 16th February 1963. This locomotive was allocated to York at the time of this photograph so it is very likely that the train originated from there. *Neville Simms*

Another picture taken on Cup Final day in 1963. The morning light had been even better at 8.02am when the 7.15am *ex*-Leicester Central, with nicely cleaned 'Jubilee' No.45622 *Nyasaland* in charge, steamed past Charwelton station (just beyond the bridge) with its exhaust hanging in the still morning air. Railway photographers had a field day with the irresistible combination of clean locomotives and perfect weather conditions – wonderful! Sadly, the day did not go quite as well for the Leicester football fans, their team going down 3-1 to Manchester United. *Tommy Tomalin*

Charwelton station, situated about three miles north of Woodford Halse, served a hamlet amid a vast agricultural area that typified this part of rural Northamptonshire. Despite its relative isolation, Charwelton acted like a magnet for railway photographers and more pictures taken in and around the station were submitted for this album than any other location of a similar status. The station marked a minor summit in each direction and, apart from a short level section where the troughs were located, steam locomotives could be photographed working fairly hard on the modest 1 in 176 gradients that applied at this point. Enthusiasts were also attracted, no doubt, by the photographic possibilities offered as locomotives replenished their water supplies on the troughs or emerged into the daylight from the nearby Catesby tunnel, or perhaps there was a convenient public house to where they could 'adjourn' on a hot summer's day. Charwelton signal box is prominent in this picture of Stanier Class 5MT No.45301 passing with an unidentified northbound summer Saturday holiday train on 8th August 1964. The GC line was an ideal route for trains from the south coast to the Midlands and north of England which used the Banbury to Woodford Halse link. *Rodney Lissenden*

A northbound empty coal train headed by BR Standard Class 9F No.92075 has just passed through Charwelton station and approaches Catesby tunnel on 10th August 1964. The station was located, as previously noted, at the top of a minor summit in each direction and the 9F's crew could look forward to downhill gradients for the next six miles to Braunston & Willoughby. The facing points on the down line opposite the signal box provided access to the siding which can be seen branching off on the right of the picture. This led through a gate and past Charwelton Hall to an ironstone quarry a fair distance away. In order to deal with the ironstone traffic Charwelton goods yard was larger than might be expected at a similar wayside station but by the date of this picture the sidings were redundant, the quarry having been worked out.
Robin Patrick

BR Standard Class 9F No.92093 is depicted leaving Catesby tunnel and approaching Charwelton station! Note the 'steaming' ventilation shaft on the hilltop above the tunnel and smoke pouring out of the tunnel entrance after the 9F had passed through. The height of the land above the tunnel will be noted – it is sometimes said that had it not been for the apparent obstinacy of the landowner a cutting would have been constructed instead of the tunnel. The boilers of locomotives based at Annesley shed were often covered in scale due to the particularly hard water at that shed and No.92093 certainly seems to have been affected by that problem. *Robin Patrick*

No.92093 again! Catesby tunnel, which was around 1¾ miles in length, was the longest on the GC's London Extension and was built on a rising gradient of 1 in 176 against trains heading southwards. The tunnel was apparently constructed at the behest of a local landowner who objected to the railway crossing his estate but the contractors encountered little difficulty during the boring of the tunnel which was completed in little over two years. Nearby Catesby House was one of several properties used by Guy Fawkes and his fellow conspirators when they were hatching the infamous Gunpowder Plot. The GC line was famous for the heavy coal trains, universally known as 'runners' or 'windcutters', that ran between Annesley and Woodford Halse and in this picture BR Standard Class 9F No.92093, hauling a return empty working, can be seen about to disappear into the depths of Catesby tunnel on 10th September 1961; note that at least one wagon is wooden-bodied. *Graham Mallinson collection*

Photographs of trains entering or leaving the southern portal of Catesby tunnel are relatively common but, for a change, here is a shot of one emerging from the northern portal which was not quite as easy to locate. The locomotive is Gresley V2 Class 2-6-2 No.60975 which was heading a goods working on 27th June 1963; like the other V2 Class engine illustrated in this section, No.60975 was based at York so it is reasonable to assume that was where the train was bound. Famous for their staccato-like exhaust beat, these locomotives have sometimes been referred to as 'the engines that helped win the war' due to their prodigious haulage capacity which proved such a boon to the operating department on the East Coast Main Line during the Second World War. The photographer would not have heard No.60975's staccato beat, however, because the locomotive would have been quietly ambling down a very long stretch of 1 in 176 gradient that applied all of the way through the tunnel and for some miles beyond. *Tommy Tomalin*

The agony of the Great Central line. The run-down of the GC line was protracted and it had been clear since the late 1950s that BR wished to be rid of what it perceived to be an unnecessary duplicate route. So the line was systematically stripped of traffic to strengthen the case for closure which was, regrettably, a widespread tactic used in the railway industry at that time. Essential infrastructure, such as water columns, was allowed to fall into disrepair and the closure of steam locomotive servicing facilities at the London end caused particular problems, it being reported that failed locomotives were often dumped at Marylebone to await towing back to Banbury which, towards the end, had become the nearest available repair point. Sunday trains had been withdrawn in March 1963 so Saturday 3rd September 1966 was the last day of daytime services in Northamptonshire – one or two overnight newspaper trains with limited passenger accommodation ran during the early hours of 4th September. The final 8.15am Nottingham (Victoria) to Marylebone working was taken by 'Black Five' No.44872 while the last up daytime train of all, the 5.15pm *ex*-Nottingham, was powered by sister engine No.44984 which was suitably adorned with a wreath and conveyed many enthusiasts. The limelight was stolen, however, by Bulleid Pacific No.35030 *Elder Dempster Lines;* this locomotive powered a Locomotive Club of Great Britain 'last day' rail tour from London. Not many people would include the county in a list of the prettiest in England but some parts of Northamptonshire are really attractive as this picture of Catesby viaduct and its surrounding landscape of rolling hills bears ample testament. The GC's London extension was famous for the grand scale of many civil engineering features, many being constructed in distinctive blue brick which was a hallmark of the line. The 12-arch Catesby viaduct was one of the most impressive on the route and took the line across the waters of the infant river Leam. In this picture Class 5MT No.45292 hurries across the viaduct with the very last 4.38pm Marylebone to Nottingham train on the evening of 3rd September 1966. When it was being built it was doubtless anticipated that the viaduct would be carrying trains for centuries to come, but in the event it achieved a useful life of only 67 years. What an appalling waste. *Neville Simms*

Woodford Halse's status as an important junction was considerably enhanced when goods trains started to run on the spur to Banbury from 1st June 1900; passenger trains began on 13th August of the same year. Goods traffic was substantial on the route right from the start and it is recorded that 60,000 wagons passed through during the first six months. In later years, coal from Nottinghamshire, fish from Grimsby and steel from Scunthorpe became staple traffic while in the reverse direction bananas from Avonmouth and endless trains of empty wagons used the line. In 1940 a peak of 689,000 loaded wagons was recorded on the link to Banbury while in 1960 the yards at Woodford were still handling around 90 trains a day, of which only about 15 were on the London line, so it is easy to see why the line to Banbury was regarded as the 'main line' with the Marylebone route as the 'branch'. While the Woodford Halse to Banbury link was vital for goods traffic and long-distance passenger services from the north to the south-west, there was also a purely local service between those locations. Sometimes nicknamed the 'Banbury Motor' this served two intermediate 'stations', Chalcombe Road Halt and Eydon Road Platform, which were closed on 6th February 1956 and 2nd April 1956 respectively. In this illustration Fairburn-designed Class 4MT 2-6-4T No.42252 stands in Woodford Halse station after arrival with the 5.48pm train from Banbury on 29th May 1964, not long before this local service was discontinued. *Tommy Tomalin*

Extract from Western Region 1961 timetable

Table 157a — BANBURY and WOODFORD HALSE

WEEK DAYS

Miles		am	pm	pm	pm (Saturdays only)	pm	pm	pm	pm (Z)	pm (Saturdays only)	pm (B)	pm (Except Saturdays)	SUNDAYS am	pm
—	Banbury .. .. dep	9 35	1218	1 50	2 44	4 20	5 48	6 0	8 3	9 20		1150	1220	6 40
11	Woodford Halse .. arr	9 55	1238	2 10	3 2	4 40	6 7	6 25	8 21	9 38		12 8	1238	6 56

WEEK DAYS

Miles		am (Z)	am (Saturdays only)	am (A)	am (Except Mondays)	am (F)	am (G)	am	pm	pm (S)	pm	pm	pm	SUNDAYS am	pm
—	Woodford Halse .. dep	1227	1256	3 10	7 44	7 50	1010		1 12	2 75	0	6 50	11 53	3 10	1215
11	Banbury .. .. arr	1245	1 14	3 34	8 8	8 8	1028		1 30	2 31	5 18	7 8	12 10	3 34	1236

A Will not run after 2nd September	F Fridays only	Z Runs Saturdays 15th July to 26th August inclusive only
a am	G Except Fridays	
B Commences 24th June	S Saturdays only	

The Woodford Halse to Banbury section was regularly visited by former GWR locomotives from Banbury shed and in this photograph 4300 Class 2-6-0 No.6378 is seen hauling a lengthy goods train towards Banbury, near Thorpe Mandeville on 12th October 1963. The delicate looking footbridge in the background carried a footpath across the line. There was a 5½ miles-long climb in the opposite direction and when the footbridge hove into view locomotive crews knew they had reached the top of the climb and the hard work was over. *R.C. Riley*

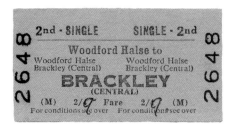

An afternoon Banbury to Woodford Halse local train, headed by Fairburn Class 4MT 2-6-4T No.42082, shuffles along near Thorpe Mandeville on the same day that the previous picture was taken; the bridge spanned a long and deep cutting. This location was particularly favoured by lineside photographers as it probably offered the best viewpoint on this unremarkable seven miles-long section. *R.C. Riley*

The county of Northamptonshire is much more closely associated with the LMSR, and to a lesser extent the LNER, than the Great Western but 'King' and 'Castle' class locomotives were a familiar sight in part of the county for decades. This was due to the fact that in the south western corner of Northamptonshire the river Cherwell formed the county border with Oxfordshire and the former GWR main line from Oxford to Banbury ran just inside the boundary for about six miles from south of the former Aynho station to approximately one mile south of Banbury. The section from Oxford to Knightcote, two miles north of Fenny Compton, was originally part of a projected route from Oxford to Rugby and was authorised by an Act on 4th August 1845, but in 1849 the GWR abandoned the idea of reaching Rugby and decided to head for the Midlands. In the meantime the Birmingham & Oxford Junction Railway (BOJR) had been authorised on 3rd August 1846 to run from the Midlands city to Knightcote where an end-on junction was envisaged with the line from Oxford. The section between Oxford and Banbury was opened on 2nd September 1850 and at first consisted of a broad gauge single line, which was doubled in 1856 and later converted to mixed gauge. The rest of the line to Birmingham, a double track, mixed gauge route, was brought into use on 1st October 1852. In this illustration 'King' Class 4-6-0 No.6025 *King Henry III,* hauling the northbound 'Cambrian Coast Express' from Paddington to Aberystwyth/Pwllheli, picks up water from Aynho troughs on 23rd June 1962. The river Cherwell can be seen on the right of the picture. *Neville Simms*

Blast off from Weedon. Towards the end of the steam era many locomotives were in a parlous condition mechanically and invariably covered with grime, so one can only imagine the reaction of the crew when they discovered they would be manning an *ex*-works BR Standard Class 9F, No.92088, which is seen here making a brisk getaway from Weedon with a chalk train to Southam cement works on Sunday 1st October 1961. The photographer recorded that the picture was taken at around 4.00pm and the soft autumn lighting, superb cloud formation, magnificent smoke effect and immaculate condition of the locomotive have combined to produce an absolute gem of a photograph. Full marks! At the time of this photograph the Weedon to Leamington Spa line had already lost its passenger trains but was still used by around half-a-dozen goods workings a day, mostly chalk trains to Southam. Regrettably, through freight working ceased in November 1962 and the 13 miles-long section from Weedon to Napton was closed from 2nd December 1963, leaving only a short stub from Leamington to provide access to the cement works. Later, a pipeline was apparently laid between the quarries, near Leighton Buzzard, and the works thus enabling the last remnant of the line to be closed. *Tommy Tomalin*

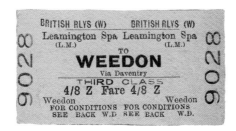

On 22nd September 1962 the South Bedfordshire Locomotive Club organised a rail tour from Luton (Bute Street) to Banbury (Merton Street) via Bletchley, a fascinating ramble over lines that had largely already lost their passenger trains or were threatened with closure; motive power was provided by former LNWR 0-8-0 No.48930 which had been spruced up for the occasion. In this picture the train is seen *en route* to Banbury at Farthinghoe, a little-photographed former junction station between Buckingham and Banbury from which passenger trains had been withdrawn on 3rd November 1952. The line from Bletchley to Banbury via Verney Junction was opened by the Buckinghamshire Railway on 1st May 1850 but never really prospered, the number of weekday trains to and from Banbury rarely exceeding five. In the mid-1950s the branch was chosen for a pilot scheme of introducing railcars to save branch lines and the service was augmented and, remarkably, two new halts were opened, so nobody could ever accuse BR of not being enterprising! Sadly, despite increased takings and a reduction in running costs the line still lost money and the passenger trains north of Buckingham succumbed to closure on 2nd January 1961. *Tommy Tomalin*

BANBURY (MERTON STREET) TO VERNEY JUNCTION

No.48930 prior to departure from Brackley Town station with the 'Banburian' rail tour on the same day the previous picture was taken. Note the manner in which people are walking casually across the track; in those days the authorities took a much more relaxed attitude compared to the stringent 'health and safety' regulations enforced today. Judging by the voluminous smoke effect, the fireman has evidently just placed quite a few shovelfuls of coal on to the fire and the train's departure was clearly imminent. This section was closed completely when goods traffic to Banbury ceased on 2nd December 1963. *Tommy Tomalin*

Hardly surprisingly, in view of the sparseness of steam workings and the route's early dieselisation, the only pictures taken on this line depict enthusiasts' specials. Here is another shot of Brackley Town station showing Fairburn Class 4MT 2-6-4T No.42105 awaiting departure with a

Railway Enthusiasts Club special on 14th September 1963. This train started from Oxford and visited Chipping Norton, Stratford-upon-Avon and Hook Norton before No.42105 took over at Banbury for a trip along the line to Verney Junction. After running round the train No.42105 proceeded to Princes Risborough from where a GWR pannier tank locomotive was motive power for a quick journey to Chinnor on the remnants of the Watlington branch, and then eventually back to Oxford. *Martin Smith*

A gloomy day at Blisworth. The fireman of Stanier Class 8F 2-8-0 No.48440 has just collected the token for the Towcester line from the signalman and rejoined the driver on the footplate, who opens up the locomotive to enable a run at a sharply-curved 1 in 171 incline that lies ahead. This picture was taken from a strategically positioned roadbridge on a very dull 3rd February 1962. Despite the closure of the passenger station in 1960, the sidings at Blisworth seem to be very busy and trains of chalk, no doubt destined for the cement works at Southam, can just be identified through the gloom. Regrettably, apart from two WCML running tracks virtually everything of railway interest in this picture has since been consigned to history and the site rendered almost unrecognisable due to the construction of the A43 dual carriageway that slices across the main line between the signal box and the former station. While the cross-country line from Blisworth to Stratford-upon-Avon and Broom Junction undoubtedly had periods of usefulness it is probably true to say its construction was almost a completely wasted effort. It was, however, one of the most fascinating routes in the area and its history has always intrigued railway historians. In 1863 the Northampton & Banbury Junction Railway (NBJR) was authorised although never reached either town, but started from the LNWR yard at Blisworth, running via Towcester to join the LNWR Verney Junction to Banbury (Merton Street) at Cockley Brake Junction. The Blisworth to Towcester section opened in June 1866 while Towcester to Cockley Brake Junction followed on 1st June 1872. The NBJR never exercised running powers over the LNWR Blisworth to Northampton line. Meanwhile the East & West Junction Railway (EWJR) had been authorised in 1864 to construct a line from Towcester to Stratford-upon-Avon, a link to Worcester having been abandoned. In 1864 Lady Palmerston, a local landowner, ceremonially cut the first sod to the accompaniment of the usual pomp and flag waving local folk; her husband, the Prime Minister, was in attendance. But within two years the funds had evaporated, work ceased and it was only due to the goodwill of creditors that the line was able to open throughout on 1st July 1873. The company's trains ran over the NBJR's metals between Blisworth and Greens Norton Junction, just west of Towcester. It was rumoured that the company's receipts were insufficient to cover the cost of oil for the locomotives and if ever a railway line was a hopeless case this was it! The EWJR was effectively bankrupt by mid-1877 and services, such as they were, ceased for eight years. Undeterred, the EWJR floated other companies in 1879 with the aim of extending from Stratford-upon-Avon to Broom Junction and from Towcester to Ravenstone Wood Junction, near Olney, on the Northampton to Bedford branch; these extensions were prompted by the discovery of vast iron ore deposits in the area. The latter, opened on 13th April 1891, proved an unmitigated financial disaster, and carried passenger trains between Olney and Towcester from only 1st December 1892 until 30th March 1893 when the service was withdrawn due to lack of patronage: it was said that some trains carried no passengers at all. In 1901 an Act was passed by Parliament authorising the sale of these small independent companies to one of the major railway companies operating in the area such as the LNWR or the GWR. Perhaps it was not surprising that none was interested and in 1908 they amalgamated as the Stratford-upon-Avon & Midland Junction Railway (SMJR); the NBJR joined in 1910. *Tommy Tomalin*

This distinctive signal box at Blisworth, which dated from 1921, controlled movements on the Towcester line until 31st October 1955 when it was downgraded to a ground frame. This photograph was taken on 29th July 1963. *The late H W Robinson / Neville Simms collection.*

The SMJR survived until The Grouping in 1923 when it was swallowed up by the LMSR. The exterior of the former station building at Towcester is depicted in this picture which was taken on 29th May 1960; this served as the headquarters of the SMJR until they were moved to Stratford-upon-Avon in about 1908. Note that the poster boards carry the initials of the LMS. During the closing years of Towcester station two passenger services operated, one from Blisworth to Banbury while the other ran from Blisworth to Stratford-upon-Avon. Both comprised two weekday trains in each direction but it should be noted that on Saturdays an extra train ran to Stratford and vice versa. The former service ran for the last time on 30th June 1951 while trains on the Stratford-upon-Avon line lasted a little longer until they, too, were axed on 7th April 1952. *Tommy Tomalin*

This panoramic view, looking north eastwards, of the former Towcester station was taken on 20th July 1958 and shows the Blisworth line immediately to the left of the signal box while the route towards Ravenstone Wood Junction and Olney is on the right; the latter had been closed completely on 28th June 1958 after it had been severed by construction work for the M1 motorway. This illustration provides an excellent view of the facilities at Towcester with the goods shed and cattle pens on the right, but the waiting shelter on the island platform had disappeared by the date of this picture. Note that six years after the last passenger train departed the station premises still present a neat and tidy appearance.
John Langford

The ruins of Towcester station. The line to Banbury diverged from the 'main line' to Stratford-upon-Avon at Greens Norton Junction, just over a mile west of Towcester station, and to simplify operations the routes were operated as two separate single lines, thus enabling the signal box at Greens Norton to be abolished. Here, Stanier Class 8F 2-8-0 No.48305 gingerly passes through the former station with a short van train from Blisworth on 10th February 1962. The top of the station building's gable can just be seen above the locomotive's tender so a lot of the old infrastructure was still in place...but for how much longer? *Neville Simms*

The rather fine signal box at Towcester had 50 levers and is believed to date from 1910 when it replaced two old signal boxes located at each end of the station layout. The signalmen at Towcester may not have been particularly busy but Easter Mondays, when the Grafton Hunt steeplechases were run, was an exception and as many as 8,000 racegoers used the station; these specials lasted until the outbreak of the Second World War. This shot of the rather elegant and imposing signal box was taken on 29th May 1960. It is understood to have continued in use until local goods and ironstone traffic was withdrawn in February 1964. *Tommy Tomalin*

Despite the withdrawal of passenger trains eleven years earlier Towcester signal box still functioned and this vintage wooden bracket signal apparently remained in everyday use at the south end of the station. The centre post seems to have lost its finial at some time so the signal looks rather odd, but what a relic! In about 1901 an Act was passed authorising the sale of the small companies that operated through Towcester to one of the much larger companies but, as previously stated, none was interested. This did not, however, stop them from using the lines for their own benefit, for example, for 30 years the MR ran goods trains between St Pancras (Somers Town) and Bristol; they also routed banana specials via the SMJR. The LNWR ran Shakespeare specials over the line and even opened a hotel at Stratford-upon-Avon in 1931. *R.C. Riley*

A rail tour leaves Towcester behind Class B12 4-6-0 No.61572 on 5th October 1963. Some of the enthusiasts leaning out of the carriage windows may have thought that their train was travelling on the wrong line but, as previously mentioned, the Stratford-upon-Avon and Banbury routes were operated between Towcester and the former Greens Norton Junction as two separate single lines as an economy measure. One of the participants appears to be taking a quick shot of the photographer! No.61572 had been officially withdrawn from traffic in October 1961 and sold for preservation so, presumably, special permission must have been given for its employment on this tour. *R.C. Riley*

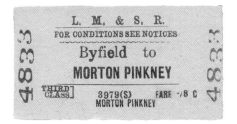

A passenger working at Byfield more than eleven years after regular passenger trains ceased! Despite the passage of time since closure, Byfield station still seems to be more or less intact, albeit somewhat weather-beaten, and the signal box certainly appears to have been manned on 5th October 1963, the day this picture was taken. The line was still regularly used at this time by freight trains, especially ironstone workings to and from various quarries in the area, the goods yard at Byfield being in use until 4th May 1964. The train was a rail tour from London powered by former LNER Class B12 4-6-0 No.61572, a particularly attractive and iconic locomotive that was, mercifully, saved from the scrap heap and at the time of writing is based on the North Norfolk Railway. *Tommy Tomalin*

There was no obvious route for a railway between London and Birmingham: various ideas were put forward and the advice of George Stephenson was sought. He favoured a route via Coventry, and Stephenson and his son were appointed joint engineers but in practice Robert did most of the detailed work. Understandably, the Lords of the Manors in Northamptonshire vociferously opposed the very thought of a railway line passing through their estates and there was also a measure of opposition in the town of Northampton, though this has tended to be over–stated. The London & Birmingham Railway Company (LBR) pressed ahead and on 23rd October 1830 Robert Stephenson recommended a line of route 4½ miles west of Northampton, but this would have to pass through 'high tracts of ground' at Blisworth and Kilsby, and the Company explored other options in the hope of reducing construction costs. It was decided that there was no practical alternative and in October 1831 Robert Stephenson advised the directors accordingly. The Company's Bill began its passage through Parliament in February 1832 but was roundly defeated in the House of Lords where the Northamptonshire landowners had considerable influence. The Bill's opponents later relented when the LBR offered increased compensation and the Bill received the Royal assent on 6th May 1833. Construction of the LBR started in November 1833, the first section from London to Denbigh Hall (Bletchley) being completed in stages and opening on 9th April 1838; passenger trains commenced between Rugby and Birmingham on the same date. The delay in opening the line throughout was caused by the heavy earthworks needed at Roade, where excavation of a deep cutting was causing difficulties, and Kilsby, where boring the 1 mile 666 yards-long tunnel was proving to be a nightmare. The contract price for construction of the tunnel was £98,988 and some problems with water penetration were anticipated but proved much more serious than first thought, and for eight months 2,000 gallons of water per minute had to be pumped out, day and night. Regrettably, 26 men lost their lives during the building of the tunnel and, in addition, the contractor went bankrupt and died, leaving the LBR to complete the task. Not surprisingly, the total cost escalated and the final bill was £291,030, almost three times the original estimate. Despite these vicissitudes the LBR opened throughout on 17th September 1838 with a full service of six trains each way (a limited service had run since 24th June) with all except the Night Mail calling at Blisworth for Northampton. Expresses from Euston took 3hr 11min to reach Blisworth and the single fare was 18s 6d (92½p.) first class. In this portrait a civil engineer's train heads southwards through Roade behind Stanier Class 8F No.48318 on 12th August 1961. *Edwin Wilmshurst*

Super power at Roade! The 9F Class 2-10-0s are generally regarded to be among the most successful, perhaps *the* most successful, of the BR Standard designs with sufficient power to haul single-handed the majority of the goods trains being operated by BR. The use of double-headed 9Fs was, therefore, extremely unusual but in this picture a brace of them, Nos.92106 and 92115, is seen passing Roade signal box with the 10.45am Gowers sidings, near Leighton Buzzard, to Southam cement works chalk train on 20th July 1964. The photographer comments that a single 8F Class 2-8-0 or 9F was normally diagrammed for this train. The Bletchley crews are looking up at the signalman who will be giving them a hand signal tip that the starting signal at the north end of the station, which they would be unable to see, was in the 'off' position. This train would have diverged from the West Coast Main Line (WCML) at Weedon. *Robin Patrick*

Photographed on the freezing cold morning of 24th January 1964, Stanier Class 5MT 4-6-0 No.45229, hauling a football special, is depicted at Roade. The train, which was identified by its reporting number displayed on the smokebox door, was conveying Fulham supporters to a match at Turf Moor, Burnley. The track and other lineside equipment was covered in frost while the locomotive's exhaust hangs in the cold morning air. *Robin Patrick*

In the mid-1960s the WCML was in the throes of electrification and in order to reduce line occupancy the 12.55pm Broad Street to Carlisle and 2.18pm Camden to Sighthill (Glasgow) fitted freight trains were sometimes combined as far as Rugby. This led to some interesting 'double headers' and in this picture, taken on 14th May 1964, BR Standard 'Britannia' Pacific Nos.70023 *Venus* and 70020 *Mercury* make a fine sight as they head past Roade. Unfortunately from the photographer's point of view the leading locomotive is in dirty condition while the train engine appears to be quite clean. This is probably explained by the fact that No.70020 was being used on rail tours during that year and its home shed, Willesden, was probably making a special effort to keep it in pristine condition. The photographer appears to have been lucky to be by the lineside whenever a particularly interesting working appeared but, actually, he was in a very privileged position being employed at Roade Junction signal box as an assistant controller from 1963 until its closure on 27th September 1964. The controller's job was an important reporting position between Euston and Rugby district controls so he

always knew if any exceptional working was around. In addition, the Roade signalman's role in regulating traffic was also vital, bearing in mind the quadruple track main line from Euston ended there with two tracks going to Northampton and two direct to Rugby via Weedon. Roade Junction was restricted to 15mph and was replaced in the 1970s by the 70mph Hanslope Junction a few miles further south. *Robin Patrick*

The same combined trains are seen again, this time on 30th July 1964, but with a slightly different combination of motive power. The train engine is Stanier 'Jubilee' 4-6-0 No.45672 *Anson* while the pilot is the doyen of the BR Standard Pacifics, No.70000 *Britannia*, which is in quite grubby condition while *Anson* appears to be smartly turned out, no doubt to the photographer's frustration once again. A few weeks before this picture was taken No.45672 made history when it worked down to Newhaven on the south coast. The locomotive subsequently failed and retired to Eastbourne shed where it was eventually patched up and turned out to work a special train from there to Haywards Heath. The SR operating authorities eventually realised the class was banned on the Brighton line and impounded *Anson*; there was considerable delay before it returned home to the LMR at reduced speed. *Robin Patrick*

The 7.45am Swanbourne (on the Bletchley to Oxford line) to Corby mineral train, powered by WD Class 2-8-0 No.90718, makes steady progress through Roade on 22nd July 1964. This working travelled via Blisworth, Northampton Bridge Street and Wellingborough over a route which is now mostly just a memory. No.90718 was constructed by Vulcan Foundry and was out-shopped in March 1945, just before the end of the Second World War; it ran as War Department No.79281 for a while before entering BR stock in December 1948. A total of 934 of these locomotives was built by the North British Locomotive Co. and Vulcan Foundry, and many served overseas as part of the war effort. No.90718 lasted in BR service until it was withdrawn in February 1966. *Robin Patrick*

In this scene recorded at Roade on 31st May 1957 Stanier 'Jubilee' Class 6P5F 4-6-0 No.45738 *Samson* is depicted charging through the station on the up fast line; *Samson* was allocated to Bushbury shed for many years so it is possible that this train was a Wolverhampton to Euston express. In the 1959 summer timetable Roade had an infrequent and irregular service which was hardly likely to attract many customers; most services were Euston to Northampton or Rugby and *vice versa* stopping trains which took an average of two hours for the journey to or from London. In the northbound direction there was a total of nine trains a day with the first being at 6.46am while the last was 9.01pm. There were very long gaps during the middle of the day: for example, between 9.50am and 4.28pm only one train was booked to stop. Roade station was closed to passenger traffic from 7th September 1964. A bridge just south of the station carried the Stratford-upon-Avon and Midland Junction Railway (SMJR) over the WCML. *RCTS Photo Archive*

There was a regular flow of heavy chalk trains from a quarry near Leighton Buzzard to the Rugby Cement works at Southam, on the branch from Weedon to Leamington Spa. The passenger service on that line was withdrawn from 15th September 1958, from which date Weedon station was also closed, but goods traffic on the branch remained buoyant and in the early 1960s it was reported that six or seven heavy freight trains traversed the line daily, mostly to and from the cement works. In this splendid landscape shot, taken north of Weedon station during the afternoon of Sunday 1st October 1961, BR Standard Class 9F No.92103 had arrived from Southam with a rake of empty chalk wagons and shunted into a siding to collect further wagons before setting off to Leighton Buzzard. Unfortunately, through goods workings ended on the branch in November 1962 and the section between Weedon and Napton (just east of Southam) was closed completely on 2nd December 1963, the chalk trains apparently being replaced by a pipeline from the quarry. A short section of the Grand Union canal is just visible on the left of the picture. *Tommy Tomalin*

A further view of the train portrayed in the previous picture, showing No.92103 heading up the main line through the former Weedon station, no doubt *en route* to the quarry with the empty wagons. Despite closure three years previously Weedon station appears to be in quite tidy condition but, of course, shorn of all identification. BR spent a fair sum modernising Weedon station, and also neighbouring Castlethorpe, a few years before they were closed; note the relatively new waiting shelters on both platforms. The platform in the foreground is a bay, complete with a run-round loop, used by pull-push trains to Daventry and Leamington Spa until they were withdrawn. In the background the photographer's 1938 vintage Rover car can be seen. *Tommy Tomalin*

The Class 9F locomotive seen in the previous two illustrations may have been in disgraceful external condition, which was typical of most BR steam power at that time, but not all engines ran around in a filthy state. In this shot No.92088, which had clearly just been released from main works, is absolutely pristine and the locomotive presents a splendid sight with shining paintwork as it poses at the head of a raft of loaded chalk tippler wagons, also on 1st October 1961. No doubt the superb condition of No.92088 made the photographer's day, but one wonders how long it remained so clean. *Tommy Tomalin*

On 30th December 1830 a meeting took place at the White Horse Inn, Towcester. Those attending included some of Northamptonshire's landed gentry and clergy who were vehemently opposed to the idea of a railway and they were led by the influential Duke of Grafton. The meeting passed three resolutions which stated, in effect, that the railway would do great harm to their estates and, in any case, the existing daily coaches and canals provided more than adequate means of transport. Initially, there was also a measure of opposition in the town of Northampton but this quickly evaporated. Robert Stephenson, the engineer in charge of the proposed London to Birmingham line, wished to avoid 'parks and pleasure grounds' and was concerned that a line through Northampton would pass close to Althorp, the seat of Earl Spencer whose son was then Chancellor of the Exchequer. He was also aware that if a route via Northampton was chosen there would be steep gradients due to the town being located in the Nene valley and the inadequate locomotives then available might not have been able to cope with the inclines. So there were sound political and geographical reasons why the route should by-pass the town and he recommended a line 4½ miles to the west. Despite the attitude of hostile landowners in February 1832 the London & Birmingham Railway (LBR) sought parliamentary approval for their line but the bill was defeated and the company had to think again. They resolved to persuade their opponents that their fears were unfounded, offered generous compensation, and eventually won the grudging support of their critics. The Bill received the Royal Assent in May 1833, Stephenson's route was approved and Northampton was destined to be served by a short branch from Blisworth, this opening on 13th May 1845. Some years later there was considerable agitation in Northampton for improved railway connections and in 1859 a public meeting in the town, chaired by the Mayor, demanded fast, through trains to London. In 1875 the LNWR, successors to the LBR, obtained powers to quadruple the main line northwards from Bletchley, and it was proposed that the two new tracks would diverge from the main line just north of Roade and continue to Rugby via Northampton and the Althorp valley. The new line joined the Market Harborough branch at Castle station by means of a very tight curve and diverged at Kingsthorpe. Castle station was rebuilt, the river diverted for half a mile, while the castle ruins were demolished to make room for a goods shed. The route opened throughout on 3rd April 1882 and at long last Northampton obtained a decent, main line service. The original main line threaded a 1½ miles-long, 65 feet deep cutting north of Roade and it is said that over one million cubic yards of spoil were removed by navvies; retaining walls more than two feet thick were required. In 1875 the LNWR deepened the cutting to accommodate the new Northampton line and lengthened the retaining walls, but there was a bad slip in November 1891 following heavy rain and iron girders were then placed across the Northampton line to hold back the walls and prevent a recurrence. The girders are on the left behind the photographer in this view of BR Standard Class 4MT 4-6-0 No.75028 as it heads towards Northampton on 15th August 1963; the main line tracks to the north are on the right. *Tommy Tomalin*

THE NORTHAMPTON LOOP LINE

Northampton, as previously mentioned, lies in a dip and southbound trains from Castle station face a difficult start, first of all on a very tight curve immediately after leaving the station and then a five miles-long, 1 in 200 climb away from the river Nene valley. About 1½ miles south of Castle station the line passes beneath an area of high ground, Hunsbury Hill, by means of a 1,152 yards-long tunnel. In this photograph, taken on a sunny evening, Class 8F 2-8-0 No.48180, is shown leaving Hunsbury Hill tunnel on 28th August 1962. One can only imagine the deafening exhaust noise being emitted by the locomotive as it heaved its heavy train up the 1 in 200 incline. *Tommy Tomalin*

Another shot taken of a train climbing away from Northampton, but this time the subject is a passenger working, the 4.13pm Wolverhampton (High Level) to Euston, and the motive power is Stanier 'Royal Scot' Class 7P 4-6-0 No.46165 *The Ranger (12th London Regt.).* This scene was recorded immediately south of Hunsbury Hill tunnel on 8th August 1962. In the summer 1963 timetable, at the height of the WCML electrification work, this train left Wolverhampton at 4.15pm and was due off Northampton at 6.25pm; the advertised arrival time in London was at 7.56pm. *Tommy Tomalin*

A field just south of Duston West signal box provided an excellent, unobstructed vantage point from where to observe trains climbing the 1 in 200 incline towards Hunsbury Hill tunnel and this location attracted generations of spotters and photographers. Here, Stanier 'Princess Coronation' Class 8P Pacific No.46241 *City of Edinburgh,* powering the 4.15pm Wolverhampton (High Level) to Euston, leaves an impressive exhaust trail in the still, evening air as it accelerates up the gradient towards Roade on 14th April 1962. When this picture was taken this legendary class was still intact but the first withdrawals occurred towards the end of 1962 and a substantial number were taken out of traffic during the following year. No.46241 survived almost to the end of the class, not being withdrawn until August 1964. *Ron Gammage*

Another London-bound express gets into its stride past Duston West signal box on 24th April 1962; motive power is provided by Stanier 'Princess Royal' Class 8P Pacific No.46206 *Princess Marie Louise*. In early 1961 increasing dieselisation on the WCML resulted in the entire 'Princess Royal' class being put into store as 'surplus to requirements' at various sheds, and this particular locomotive was stored at Rugby. During the summer most engines were returned to service and No.46206 was allocated to Crewe North shed for the duration of the summer timetable; its nameplates, which had been removed for safe keeping, were re-instated. After a brief spell of activity the class was, once again, put into storage and No.46206 found itself back at Rugby; six members of the class were withdrawn during September. In early 1962 there was a motive power shortage and the remaining six locomotives were returned to steam, working front line WCML express services as far north as Perth. This charmed life could not last forever and the surviving members of this celebrated class were withdrawn in September with the exception of No.46200 *The Princess Royal* which continued at work for a few more weeks. *Ron Gammage*

The following three pictures were taken from a window of Duston West signal box and illustrate the wonderful variety of steam motive power that could be observed in the late 1950s and early 1960s. In this portrait, taken on 7th May 1959, 7F Class 0-8-0 No.49431 plods up the incline towards Hunsbury Hill tunnel with a long goods train in tow; the long buildings behind the locomotive are the old carriage sheds. This locomotive was originally constructed at Crewe by the London & North Western Railway (LNWR) as a G2 class and this particular example emerged from the works there in July 1922. This type was the mainstay of the LNWR's freight operation and was the only class of that company's locomotives to survive into BR ownership in any significant number; No.49431 was destined to remain in service until late 1962. *Ron Gammage*

THE NORTHAMPTON LOOP LINE

The Hughes/Fowler Class 6P5F 2-6-0s, which were universally nicknamed 'Crabs', tended to be more common in the north of England than in the more southerly parts of LMR territory – there was even a sizeable allocation in Scotland. So it is likely, therefore, that the photographer was pleasantly surprised when No.42777, in quite presentable external condition, hove into view on a southbound goods working. This locomotive was based at Crewe South shed at the time of the photograph, one of around a dozen allocated to that depot. No.42777 was built at Crewe and emerged from the works in August 1927 and lasted almost forty years in service before being withdrawn in August 1965. *Ron Gammage*

The main line to Roade is carried on a curving embankment for the first mile or so immediately south of Northampton (Castle) station; it crosses the river Nene on a 15-arch viaduct and the Grand Union canal on a high girder bridge. In happier days, when the town's railway system was still intact, this route also passed over the branch from Duston West junction to Blisworth, this being the original 'main line' to and from London before the route to Roade was built. In this portrait BR Standard Class 9F 2-10-0 No.92132, in charge of a long coal train, crosses over the canal and Blisworth line at Duston West on 17th May 1962; the distant rooftops and factory chimneys of Northampton provide the backdrop. Part of the 15-arch viaduct over the river can be seen beyond the yellow speed restriction board; the viaduct parapet was being rebuilt at the time and the new brickwork can just be discerned. The course of the river Nene is hidden by the embankment on the right of the picture. *Ron Gammage*

Stanier 'Princess Coronation' Pacific No.46221 *Queen Elizabeth* 'blows off' as it crosses the 15-arch viaduct that takes the railway across the river Nene, which is just visible on the left of the picture. This portrait was taken on 7th May 1959. The viaduct was undergoing partial reconstruction at the time – note the scaffolding and hoist on the left – and a temporary speed restriction was in force. No.46221 was one of a batch of five locomotives out-shopped from Crewe works in 1937 for working the prestigious 'Coronation Scot' train from London to Glasgow which was launched to compete with the LNER's 'Flying Scotsman'. When built No.6221 (as it then was) would have been streamlined and painted in a striking blue livery with horizontal silver bands. Many experts consider these locomotives to be the finest express passenger engines ever to run in Great Britain and in 1937 the doyen of the class, No.6220 *Coronation*, attained a maximum speed of 114mph just south of Crewe, breaking the (then) speed record for steam traction. Two years later No.6229 *Duchess of Hamilton* exchanged identities with No.6220 *Coronation* and was exhibited at the New York World's Fair. It was stranded in the United States due to the outbreak of the Second World War; it reverted to its original identity when it returned home in 1943. *Ron Gammage*

On Sunday 23rd September 1962 the main line to Roade was blocked for work on the permanent way and here Hughes/Fowler Class 6P/5F 2-6-0 No.42856 and Stanier Class 8F No.48376 simmer on the viaduct across the river Nene which was locally known to the railway enthusiast fraternity as '15 arches'. The former locomotive was allocated to Stoke shed at the time while the 8F was a Kettering engine so, presumably, both had been borrowed for the day by Northampton shed. The engine crews were no doubt grateful for the overtime, especially bearing in mind they probably did not have a great deal to do, apart from ensuring the locomotive's fires did not go out! By the date of this picture the quite extensive work on the viaduct appears to have been finished, the new brickwork being clearly visible. *Graham Onley*

A view of the track layout at the south end of Northampton (Castle) station on the snowy morning of 16th March 1964. The main line to Roade curves round to the right past Northampton corporation's refuse destructor plant, on the right of the shot in the middle background. The line going straight ahead bifurcates at Duston North Junction, about half a mile to the south, the route to the east serving Wellingborough and Bedford while the line to the west soon changes direction to run due south to Blisworth. The carriage sheds can be discerned beyond Northampton No.1 signal box while the canopy in the foreground hides the old bay platforms that were used by branch trains. Northampton engine shed was located in a triangle formed by the Wellingborough and Blisworth routes and the spur that connected them which enabled through running between those locations. The plume of steam in the middle of the photograph indicates the shed's location. *Graham Onley*

Car park full! The car park at Northampton (Castle) station did not appear to be anything like full when this picture was taken on 3rd October 1962 because there was a one day rail strike on that day and also somebody seems to have forgotten to turn off the gas lamps... perhaps that was a consequence of the strike. Oh dear, what a way to run a railway station! The old station's frontage was reasonably elegant and in times past its elegance was enhanced by an attractive port-cochère which was no doubt appreciated on a rainy day when ladies were alighting from their carriages. Between 1965 and 1967 it was reconstructed in typical 1960s uninspiring 'steel and glass' style in connection with electrification of the WCML and has been rebuilt once again as if to stress the inadequacy of the 1960s-era building. *Graham Onley*

'What, no trains', may well have been the reaction of passengers unaware of the strike action when arriving at Northampton (Castle) station on 3rd October 1962, the same day that the previous picture was taken. At least this photograph gives an excellent view of the old, somewhat dilapidated premises, looking northwards from the southbound platform. Note the water crane, a symbol of the steam age if ever there was one, signs in the London Midland Region standard maroon colour, and oil tail lamps on the platform. A Wymans bookstall can just be discerned on the extreme right of the picture while piles of parcels on barrows litter the platform – a reminder of the days when parcels traffic was a substantial source of income on the railways. Out of sight on the right are two bay platforms used by local trains to and from the north. *Graham Onley*

A photograph taken about 2¼ miles north of Northampton (Castle) station at 6.20pm on 17th May 1962, which appears to have been a lovely spring day. The 4.25pm Euston to Wolverhampton train, powered by BR Standard Class 5MT 4-6-0 No.73014, regains momentum after slowing for a speed restriction across the river bridge in the background which was under repair. Northampton, as previously mentioned, lies in a valley and trains bound for Rugby face a continuous climb at 1 in 230 for about nine miles until Long Buckby is reached. In times gone by there were a number of intermediate stations between Northampton and Rugby but Long Buckby is the only one that survives today. Church Brampton closed as long ago as May 1931 while Althorp Park, which was provided primarily to serve the neighbouring estate, closed from 13th June 1960; Kilsby & Crick was closed during the same year, from 1st February. *Tommy Tomalin*

A large mass of dark cloud hovers nearby and the photographer appears to have been very fortunate with the sun which is shining brightly on Stanier Class 8F 2-8-0 No.48615 as it descends from Long Buckby towards Northampton with an enormously long goods train. This portrait was taken on 25th November 1961 south of the former station of Church Brampton. *Tommy Tomalin*

Northampton shed was built in typical LNWR style and had ten, single-ended roads and a northlight pattern roof. The early history of the shed is unclear but it seems that an engine shed was erected in the 1850s and subsequently enlarged in 1870. In 1881 a new shed was constructed in the triangle of lines south of Castle station adjacent to the Grand Union canal; this shed could house a maximum of 40 locomotives. It seems that for many years Northampton shed had spare capacity and despite inheriting locomotives based at the MR's Hardingstone Lane shed in the town, which closed on 1st October 1924, its allocation in 1925 was only 36 engines. A new 60ft turntable was installed in 1938 and a water softening plant erected at the same time. BR planned to modernise the shed but improvements, which included new coal and ash plants, were delayed until 1952. In the 1950s the depot's stock rose and largely consisted of goods classes, including LMSR Class 4F 0-6-0s, LNWR 0-8-0s and 8F 2-8-0s; in addition there was a small stud of 'Black Fives' for important passenger work and tank engines for local duties. The electrification of the WCML was the deathknell for Northampton shed which closed from 27th September 1965 but three 'Jinty' 0-6-0Ts survived on local duties almost to the end. The shed was hardly a Mecca for express passenger locomotives but occasionally a really exceptional engine appeared such as named Stanier Class 5MT No.45156 *Ayrshire Yeomanry* which was photographed on 19th May 1963; a converted Crosti-boilered Class 9F is also just visible. The 'Black Five' was based at Newton Heath shed, Manchester, at the time and was one of only two named members of the class to be allocated to an English depot. *Ron Gammage*

A Sunday was always the best day of the week to visit a steam shed, particularly if you did not possess the necessary authorisation and risked being ejected by an irate foreman! There was also the prospect of spotting many more locomotives: after all, it was the quietest day of the week and most of the engines would be 'on shed'. On Sunday 12th April 1964 the photographer discovered Stanier 'Jubilee' Class 6P/5F 4-6-0 No.45556 *Nova Scotia* lurking in the depths of Northampton motive power depot and, luckily, well placed for a quick portrait. This may have been *Nova Scotia's* last visit to the shed because it was withdrawn four months later. Enthusiasts visiting on that day would have been rewarded by the sight of another 'Jubilee', No.45655 *Keith,* and BR Standard 'Britannia' Pacific Nos.70021 *Morning Star* and No.70023 *Venus.* The atmosphere of a working steam shed, with its almost magical aroma of sulphur, steam and hot oil, is something the preservation movement has struggled to re-create. *Graham Onley*

The dying days of Northampton shed. The depot is seen here on the morning of 6th June 1965 with just eight locomotives in view comprising Stanier Class 5MTs and 8Fs – quite a contrast to more prosperous days. On the extreme left of the picture a small section of the Grand Union canal can be discerned while beyond is the viaduct carrying the line from Bridge Street junction to Duston North junction. *Graham Onley*

A landmark in the history of Northampton shed was the installation of a new 60ft turntable in 1938 which is depicted in this shot taken in September 1965 during the last few days of steam operation. Truly the end of an era. Stanier Class 5MT No.45190, an Armstrong Whitworth product built in October 1935, lasted in service for almost another three years and was eventually taken out of service in May 1968, shortly before the curtain came down on BR steam.
Ron Gammage

The coaling plant looks remarkably clean and modern and indeed it was, having been constructed, together with an ash plant, in 1952 as previously mentioned. The latter is out of the picture, concealed from view by the giant 'coaler' which was no doubt an unwelcome landmark in this part of the town. One wonders what local people thought perhaps they regarded it as an intrusive monstrosity, but those who worked for BR were perhaps a good deal more understanding. This picture was taken on an unknown date in 1965 and, judging by the total lack of activity, the shed may have been closed but at least a coal supply was still available. On the distant horizon electrification masts on the line to Euston can just be seen so this picture gives a good idea of the position of the shed in relation to the main line. Sadly, everything of railway interest in this shot, apart from the Euston line, has been obliterated. *Robin Patrick*

The 18 miles-long Northampton to Market Harborough line was designed and built by George Stephenson for the LNWR which obtained an Act of Parliament authorising construction in 1853. When the line first opened, on 16th February 1859, it started at Duston West Junction because the main Roade to Rugby line via Northampton had not yet been built. The Northampton to Market Harborough line converged with the LNWR's Rugby to Peterborough route at Market Harborough but, curiously, was operated as a self-contained branch until the LMSR laid a connection with the former MR main line in 1924. The route, which served an agricultural area with little population, originally had six stations but Spratton was an early casualty closing from 23rd May 1949 while Pitsford & Brampton lasted until 5th June 1950. There were two tunnels, near Kelmarsh, and Oxendon stations, both having two separate bores with different lengths, quite an unusual feature for a branch of this nature.

Unfortunately, many of the intermediate stations were located at road crossings, some of which were a considerable distance from the villages they purported to serve and the local buses were no doubt a more convenient proposition for villagers. The summer 1959 timetable advertised a mere six local trains in each direction on weekdays only, the crack, long distance express being a summer Saturday Leicester to Eastbourne/Hastings holiday train which did not, of course, stop intermediately. The line was closed to local passenger traffic from 4th January 1960, but was temporarily reopened for diverted through passenger trains for five months in 1969 and for just over a year from July 1972; it continued to be used for such trains sporadically for some time afterwards. The line was very steeply graded and heavy goods trains were banked from Market Harborough to Kelmarsh, which was situated 400 feet above sea level, and in the late 1950s this duty was shared by Class 7F 0-8-0s Nos.49444 and 49447. When they were transferred to Springs Branch (Wigan) shed in August 1960 visiting locomotives normally undertook this chore, the most frequent performers being WD Class 2-8-0s. The last local trains on the line were the 8.33pm Northampton (Castle) to Market Harborough and 9.30pm return on 2nd January 1960. The former consisted of five coaches hauled by Ivatt Class 2MT 2-6-2T No.41218 but this developed a fault and was unable to power the return working which was taken by Fowler 2-6-4T No.42331, so it turned out to be quite an eventful last day with revellers arriving back in Northampton nearly an hour late. The most interesting goods workings over the line were probably the hopper trains that ran between the Nottinghamshire coalfield and Stonebridge Park power station that provided traction current for the LMR's north London suburban electric trains. Here, Stanier 8F Class 2-8-0 No.48312 heads north in the evening sunshine with an empty train on 17th May 1963; it is seen about a mile from Northampton (Castle) station. *Tommy Tomalin*

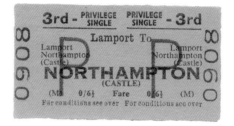

A local bus just creeps into this picture of Boughton crossing – it is partially visible on the extreme right of the shot. The bus was probably heading to the village of Boughton which was located just over a mile away, a distance that would have deterred all but the most determined railway passenger. The local buses in this area, as previously mentioned, proved to be the undoing of local passenger services on routes radiating from Northampton. The train, headed by BR Standard Class 9F No.92049, is a similar working to that seen in the previous photograph; note the very distinctive hopper wagons. This portrait was taken on the evening of 27th May 1964. *Tommy Tomalin*

A southbound coal train, headed by Stanier Class 8F 2-8-0 No.48545, drifts downhill through the closed station of Pitsford & Brampton on 25th August 1962. The station was sited on the side of a valley in a cutting. Here again, buses were in an ideal position to siphon off railway passengers, the village of Pitsford being more than two miles from the station so it is not surprising it was an early closure victim, as previously stated. There was a quarry at Pitsford, located a short distance south of the station on the eastern side; it opened in November 1921 and lasted until 1965. Pitsford is today the base of the Northampton and Lamport heritage railway. *Tommy Tomalin*

The gables add a decorative touch to the otherwise somewhat austere station building at Brixworth which was photographed looking southwards on 1st July 1964. Brixworth was probably the largest intermediate settlement on the Northampton to Market Harborough line and the station retained passenger facilities until the route was closed to local passenger traffic on 4th January 1960; goods traffic was handled here until 1st January 1964. Note that at least one oil lamp standard is still *in situ* more than four years after closure. *Tommy Tomalin*

A southbound coal train, headed by a reasonably clean Stanier Class 8F 2-8-0 No.48538, comes down the bank through the former Lamport station on 16th July 1964. This station also survived until the line's local passenger trains ceased despite being in an isolated location; Lamport was only a small village located less than a mile from the station. Surprisingly for such a rural wayside station, there were originally two signal boxes while a third was located at Lamport ironstone sidings about two miles south of the station; the last-mentioned closed in February 1970. There was an unusual accident at Lamport on 20th July 1957 when a coach driver was taken ill at the wheel and crashed into the crossing gates just as a light engine, WD Class 2-8-0 No.90103, was passing through the station. The locomotive's driver swiftly applied the brake but was unable to prevent a collision with the vehicle and they came to a stand side by side between the platforms. *Tommy Tomalin*

Table 62 — NORTHAMPTON AND MARKET HARBOROUGH—Weekdays only

Miles		a.m.	a.m.	SX p.m.	SO p.m.	SO p.m.			p.m.		p.m.	p.m.	p.m.	
—	50LONDON (Euston) .... dep	...	6F40	11a50	11a57	12 20			12SX2		2J50	4 25	6 55	...
0	NORTHAMPTON (Castle) ... dep	6 30	8 35	1 45	1 45	3 14			3 45		5 33	6 20	8 33	.
7¼	Brixworth	6 41	...	1 58	1 58				3 56		5 44	6 31	8 44	.
9¾	Lamport	6 46	..	2 3	2 3				4 1		5 49	6 36	8 49	.
13½	Kelmarsh	6 53	..	2 10	2 10				4 8		5 56			.
14½	Clipston and Oxendon	6 56	..	2 13	2 13				4 11		5 59	6 45	8 58	.
18	MARKET HARBOROUGH ... arr	7 3	9 0	2 20	2 20	3 42			4 18		6 6	6 52	9 5	.
34	180LEICESTER (London Road) ... arr	7 44	9H36	3 23	3 6	4 7			5 G24		7M38		9 52	

Mil		a.m.	SX a.m.	SO a.m.	a.m.	p.m.	SO p.m.	SO p.m.		p.m.		p.m.	p.m.	p.m.	
—	180LEICESTER (London Road) ... dep	6 10	8 55	8 57	10N5	12 35				2SX36		4SX36	6P34	8 45	...
—	MARKET HARBOROUGH ... dep	7 38	9 22	9 26	11 32	1 7		1D 7		3 15		5 7	7 25	9 30	...
3½	Clipston and Oxendon	7 45	9 29	9 33	11 39					3 22		5 13	7 32	9 37	...
4½	Kelmarsh		9 32	9 36	11 42					3 25		5 17		9E40	
8½	Lamport	7 53	9 38	9 42	11 48				1 43	3 31		5 23	7 40	9 46	
10½	Brixworth	7 59	9 42	9 46	11 52					3 35		5 27	7 44	9 50	
18	NORTHAMPTON (Castle) ... arr	8 16	9 53	9 57	12 3	1 43F		1 43		3 46		5 38	7 55	10 1	.
83¾	50LONDON (Euston) .... arr	10B 7	11 21	11 32	3C 40	3 40				6 20		7 42	10 58	.	

A—Arrives 3 minutes earlier.
B—5 minutes later on Saturdays.
C—On Saturdays arrives London (Euston) 3.0 p.m.
D—On 2nd August stops only to pick up passengers.
E—Stops at Kelmarsh on Saturdays. Also stops when required
    Mondays to Fridays on notice being given at Market Harborough.
F—On Mondays to Fridays departs London (Euston) 6.45 a.m.
G—On Saturdays arrives Leicester (London Road) 6.6 p.m.
H—On Saturdays arrives Leicester (London Road) 9.43 a.m.

J—On Saturdays departs London (Euston) 3.5 p.m.
M—On Saturdays arrives Leicester (London Road) 7.40 p.m.
N—On Saturdays departs Leicester (London Road) 10.22 a.m.
P—On Saturdays departs Leicester (London Road) 6.40 p.m.
SO—Saturdays only.
SX—Saturdays excepted.
TC—Through Carriage.
a—a.m.

Extract from
London Midland
Region summer
1959 timetable

An absolutely filthy BR Standard Class 9F 2-10-0, No.92078, approaches the former Kelmarsh station with a northbound empty coal train on 12th September 1964. The line is climbing quite steeply at this point and the station here was on the 400ft contour, as previously mentioned. The village of Kelmarsh is situated about a mile from the station but on a main road, so passenger traffic here was probably minimal.
Tommy Tomalin

The Northampton to Market Harborough line does not appear to have attracted many photographers and this is the only picture of a passenger train on that line submitted for consideration for this book which, of course, virtually guaranteed its inclusion! Here, Ivatt Class 2MT 2-6-2T No.41219 is depicted drawing to a halt at Clipston & Oxendon station on 28th February 1959. The station porter is waiting dutifully on the platform just in case the odd passenger deigns to alight...you never know! *John Langford*

The scene is the former station at Blisworth, three miles north of Roade, at 11.30am on a rather gloomy 3rd February 1962. Blisworth was originally the junction station for Northampton when the branch opened on 13th May 1845 as part of the route to Peterborough which opened for business throughout on 2nd June 1845. Latterly, trains on that line had run between Northampton and Peterborough (East) only, which was a 43¾ miles-long cross country ramble that connected a number of intermediate towns. The station at Blisworth had been closed from 4th January 1960 when regular passenger trains were withdrawn between there and Northampton, but it should be noted that until 3rd January 1966 this line was used by trains diverted in connection with the electrification of the WCML; towards the end this service had consisted of about seven return trains on weekdays only. Despite the closure of the station and withdrawal of passenger services to Stratford-upon-Avon many years previously, Blisworth is a hive of activity in this picture with a London-bound express rushing past on the main line and two steam locomotives visible. On the right Stanier Class 8F 2-8-0 No.48107 is blowing off impatiently as it waits for the 'road' with a long goods train. On the left a line of wagons loaded with iron ore can be seen on the former SMJR side of the station while another 8F is occupied on shunting duties. This picture was obtained by climbing onto the water tower at the south end of the former station area – could one ask for a better viewpoint? *Tommy Tomalin*

Extract from London Midland Region summer 1959 timetable

Table 73—

NORTHAMPTON AND BLISWORTH—Weekdays only.

Miles			SX a.m.	SO a.m.		a.m.	a.m.		SX a.m.	SO a.m.		SO					SO p.m.	SO p.m.					
—	50 LONDON Euston .... dep		...	...	...	6 A40	...	...	...	...	...	8a50	11B50	12C2	...	2D50	7 25	...	...	...	...	...	...
0	NORTHAMPTON Castle .... dep		6 55	7 10	...	8 15	8 40	...	10 0	10 15	...	12 17	1 35	2 43	...	5 15	9 35	10 10	.	.	.	.	.
4½	BLISWORTH .... arr		7 5	7 20	...	8 25	8 50	.	10 10	10 15	...	12 27	1 45	2 35	...	5 25	9 45	10 20	...	...	...	...	...

Miles			a.m.		SX a.m.	SO a.m.		SO p.m.		SX p.m.	SO p.m.		p.m.	SO p.m.		SO p.m.						
0	BLISWORTH .... dep		6 54	...	8 25	8 28	...	12 40	.	2 3	2 15	...	3 5	5 32	...	10 5	...	...	...	...	...	...
4½	NORTHAMPTON Castle .... arr		7 5	...	8 36	8 38	.	12 52	.	2 13	2 15	...	3 15	5 42	...	10 15	.	.	.	.	.	.
65½	50 LONDON Euston .... arr		9E45	...	10 7	...	...	3 40	...	4 15	4 15	...	6 20	7 42	...	...	...	...	...	...	...	...

A—5 minutes later on Mondays to Fridays.
B—Is a.m. On Saturdays departs 11.57 a.m.
C—On Saturdays departs 12.20 p.m.

D—On Saturdays departs 3.5 p.m.
E—4 minutes earlier on Saturdays.

SO—Saturdays only.
SX—Saturdays excepted.
a—a.m.

The irresistible combination of steam, sun and snow combine to produce a sparkling image of Stanier Class 5MT No.45331 passing Duston sidings with a short goods working on 22nd January 1963. In order to produce a particularly memorable picture an *ex*-works locomotive was thoughtfully provided by BR; what more could the photographer have wished for, a double-header perhaps! *Tommy Tomalin*

A train of iron ore, headed by converted Crosti-boiler Class 9F 2-10-0 No.92025, has just come off the Wellingborough line at Duston West Junction signal box and heads down the route towards Blisworth on 5th October 1963. The point of convergence of the lines from Northampton (Castle) station with the route from Peterborough and Wellingborough was almost directly beneath the bridge that carried the main line to London across the layout. The 9F appears to be working 'flat out' as it approaches the photographer, in complete contrast to Stanier Class 8F 2-8-0 No.48600 which is ambling along on a local goods working which had presumably originated at Blisworth. *Ron Gammage*

A very rare photograph of a steam crane in action. This picture was taken at Duston West on 23rd September 1962 when, what is understood to be, the Rugby steam crane was working on bridge deck renewal in connection with the impending electrification of the West Coast Main Line. At that time most major depots had their own crane for use on engineering works, as seen here, or at incidents such as derailments etc. Steam cranes had to be kept permanently in light steam to ensure they were available to attend an incident at very short notice. This photograph gives a good view of the junction of the Northampton and Wellingborough lines with Northampton shed's coaling plant just discernible in the far distance. The train pictured is a regular Sunday Holyhead to Broad Street working conveying meat containers which had been diverted to run along the 'old line' to Blisworth; motive power is 'Black Five' No.45044. A mineral line from Far Cotton to Duston furnaces used to pass beneath the arch on the right of the picture. *Graham Onley*

The train service on the Northampton to Peterborough line advertised in the summer 1963 timetable comprised around half a dozen trains each way on weekdays only but it should be noted that additional services operated between Northampton (Castle) and Wellingborough (Midland Road) station. Both services were officially withdrawn from 4th May 1964 but as there was no Sunday service the last trains ran on Saturday 2nd May. On that fateful day Ivatt Class 2MT 2-6-2T No.41224 is seen pulling out of Northampton (Castle) station with the 2.00pm to Wellingborough. Many of the stations on this line were inconveniently sited in relation to the places they supposedly served and consequently most passengers had long since deserted the railway for the more convenient local buses. *Ron Gammage*

A further view at the same location, but this time showing Stanier 'Black Five' No.45430 hauling an inspection saloon on 20th April 1962. The saloon is likely to have been used by the district civil engineer when carrying out inspections of the line in his area and the photographer mentions that it was kept in a shed near Bridge Street station.
Ron Gammage

A Northampton panorama. This view was taken from the footbridge leading to Northampton shed and depicts Bridge Street Junction: the main running lines in the centre of the picture are those from Blisworth while those on the left are from Northampton (Castle) station; the sidings on the right belonged to the district civil engineer. Bridge Street station can just be discerned in the centre of the picture while Northampton power station's cooling towers are prominent on the horizon. This picture was taken on 11th October 1964, by which date passenger services to Bedford and Peterborough had been withdrawn from the lines depicted. *Graham Onley*

The station nameboard on the right immediately identifies the location of this picture but the train shown here is a rail tour with a complex itinerary which certainly requires an explanation. This Stephenson Locomotive Society trip ran on 14th April 1962 and was advertised as a tour of seven branch lines – needless to say most of these have since been consigned to history. The trip started from Birmingham (New Street) with Class 2P 4-4-0 No.40646 in charge and travelled to Northampton via Nuneaton and Rugby. On arrival at Northampton (Castle) station Fowler Class 3MT 2-6-2T No.40026, one of the examples with condensing apparatus, was attached as train engine with No.40646 as pilot and the train then proceeded to Bedford where No.40646 was detached; the train then went on to Hitchin. There the services of No.40026 were dispensed with and preserved Great Northern Railway 0-6-0ST No.1247 took over for a short tour of lines in the area finishing at Luton (Bute Street) where No.40646 was waiting to haul the participants back to Birmingham via Leighton Buzzard, Daventry and Kenilworth. What an absolutely amazing day! *R.C. Riley*

Northampton Bridge Street station's attractive frontage is depicted in this portrait which was taken on 14th April 1962. The brick-built building boasts two really delightful shaped gables with stone surrounds, and the stone quoins are another decorative embellishment that enhance the appeal of the structure. Note the stonework above the canopy which gives the appearance of being a balcony. Bridge Street was the focal point of three secondary routes and was constructed many years before Castle station came onto the scene, but all of those lines fell victim to the growth of motor transport and the station closed its doors for the last time on 2nd May 1964. *Ron Gammage*

The rose garden at Bridge Street station on 19th June 1960: the other flowers appear to be lupins. The 'sausage' station sign is in mint condition and one wonders whether it was brand new or, perhaps, the station staff were particularly keen on keeping the premises looking very smart. *Tommy Tomalin*

Opposite Extract from Eastern Region summer 1960 timetable

The last years of the Wellingborough service. An immaculately turned out Ivatt Class 2MT 2-6-2T, No.41224, gathers speed through Bridge Street station with the 12.20pm from Castle station to Wellingborough Midland Road on 14th April 1962, a bright spring day. Some trains to and from Wellingborough ran non-stop and the working seen here was one of those, but services to and from Peterborough usually called at Bridge Street. This picture provides a good view of the station's ornate chimneys and stonework – what a gem. A BR parcels van and rather fine bus stand in the station yard; the latter belonged to the district civil engineer and was used to take track gangs to inaccessible locations. *Tommy Tomalin*

PETERBOROUGH, WELLINGBOROUGH and NORTHAMPTON

Week Days only

Miles		am		am		am		pm	pm	pm A	pm	pm		pm		pm	
—	**Peterborough** (East) .. dep	6 43	..	7 35	..	9 46	..	12 30	12 40	3 40	3 50	4 0	..	6 0	..	8 49	..
13¼	Oundle	7 5	..	7 56	..	10 7	..	12 51	1 1	4 11	4 21	..	..	6 21	..	9 10	..
15¾	Barnwell	7 10	..	8 1	..	10 12	..	12 56	1 6	4 16	4 26	..	..	6 26	..	9 15	..
19	Thorpe	7 16	..	8 7	..	10 18	..	1 2	1 12	4 22	4 32	..	..	6 32	..	9 21	..
21¾	Thrapston (Bridge Street) ..	7 23	..	8 12	..	10 24	..	1 8	1 18	4 29	4 38	..	..	6 40	..	9 27	..
24¾	Ringstead & Addington . . .	7 29	..	8 18	..	10 30	..	1 14	1 24	4 35	4 44	..	..	6 46	..	9 33	..
27	Irthlingborough . .	7 36	..	8 24	..	10 36	..	1 22	1 32	4 44	4 51	..	..	6 52	..	9 39	..
31¾	**Wellingborough** (London Rd.)	7 45	..	8 34	..	10 45	..	1 31	1 41	4 54	4 59	..	..	7 5	..	9 47	..
35½	Castle Ashby & Earls Barton ..	7 53	..	8 42	..	10 53	..	1 39	1 49	..	5 7	..	..	..	..	..	..
42¼	**Northampton** (Bridge St.)..	8 5	..	8 54	..	11 9	..	1 51	2 1	4 45	..	..	..	7 23	..	10 5	..
43½	" (Castle) .. arr	8 9	..	8 58	..	11 13	..	1 55	2 5	4 49	5 17	5 22	..	7 27	..	10 11	..

Week Days only

Miles		am B		am		am		pm	pm	pm	pm		pm		pm	
—	**Northampton** (Castle) .. dep	6 42	..	7 13	..	9 32	..	12 28	..	..	5 10	..	6 42	..		
1	(Bridge St.) ..	6 46	..	7 17	..	9 35	..	12 31	..	..	5 13	..	6 45	..		
8	Castle Ashby & Earls Barton	6 57	..	7 28	..	9 46	..	12 42	..	..	5 24	..	6 56	..		
12	**Wellingborough** (London Rd.)	7 6	..	7 37	..	9 54	..	12 51	..	4 21	5 37	..	7 7	..		
16¾	Irthlingborough.. . . .	7 16	..	7 46	..	10 2	..	12 59	..	4 28	5 45	..	7 15	..		
19	Ringstead & Addington	7 22	..	7 52	..	..	..	1 5	..	4 34	5 51	..	7 21	..		
22½	Thrapston (Bridge Street)	7 30	..	7 59	..	10 12	..	1 12	..	4 42	5 58	..	7 28	..		
24¾	Thorpe	7 37	..	8 6	..	10 19	..	1 19	..	4 49	6 5	..	7 35	..		
28	Barnwell	7 43	..	8 12	..	10 25	..	1 25	..	4 55	6 11	..	7 41	..		
30½	Oundle	7 50	..	8 19	..	10 31	..	1 31	..	5 2	6 17	..	7 47	..		
43	**Peterborough** (East) .. arr	8 12	..	8 41	..	10H53	..	1 53	..	..	6 39	..	8 9	..		

A Through Train from Yarmouth (Vauxhall) dep 12 41 pm and Lowestoft (Central) dep 12 28 pm (Tables 43, 5, 35)

B Through Train to Yarmouth (Vauxhall) arr 11 9 am (Tables 35, 5, 43)

H On Saturdays arrives 10 56 am

The 12.28pm Northampton (Castle) to Peterborough (East) train, with B1 Class 4-6-0 No.61095 in charge, is depicted leaving Bridge Street station on 14th April 1962. Northampton power station's massive cooling towers are partially visible on the left of the picture. *Ron Gammage*

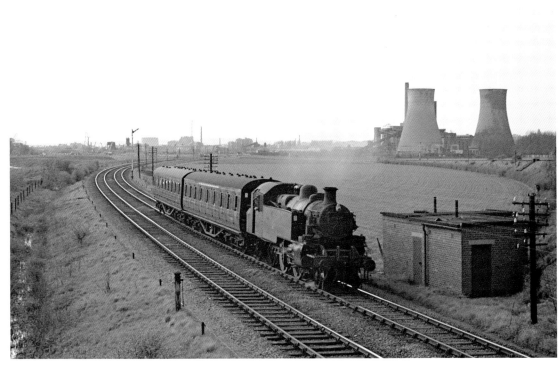

Northampton power station's cooling towers are seen again and obviously constituted a major landmark in the town which many local people probably regarded as a huge blot on the landscape that has since been removed. In this picture Ivatt Class 2MT 2-6-2T No.41227 is seen heading towards Wellingborough with a 'pull-push' train just a few days before the cessation of the service. The line on the embankment on the right of the shot is the erstwhile MR route to Bedford which lost its passenger trains from 5th March 1962. Originally trains to and from Bedford used St John's Street station which was the Midland Railway's foothold in Northampton, but this was closed from 3rd July 1939 when services were diverted to Castle station. *Robin Patrick*

Some trains on the Northampton to Wellingborough line were extended to Kettering and here the 5.35pm from Kettering, propelled by Ivatt 2-6-2T No.41224, is seen passing the derelict, grass-grown platforms of the former Billing station on 17th August 1962. Unfortunately, the station was situated in splendid isolation about two miles from the villages of Great Billing and Little Billing and the nearest habitation was actually the village of Cogenhoe, but even that was a mile away. All of these places are about five miles or so from Northampton town centre and probably reasonably well-served by buses so it was, perhaps, inevitable that Billing station saw few passengers even in the heyday of rail transport and it is surprising that it survived until 6th October 1952. *Tommy Tomalin*

Little train, big landscape. The 10.30am from Wellingborough to Northampton, with Ivatt 2-6-2T No.41219 in charge, was photographed in a delightful rural setting near Cogenhoe on the bright spring day of 8th April 1962. Note that unlike other Wellingborough trains in this section it is formed of ordinary coaching stock and not a 'pull-push' set. The train is running along the lush valley of the river Nene which the line follows as far as Wellingborough and, indeed, all of the way to Peterborough. *Tommy Tomalin*

Visitors to Wellingborough looking for London Road station could be forgiven for walking straight past this building unless, that is, they just happened to spot the signal on the left of the shot. Apart from one or two poster boards there is very little to indicate that it is a railway station. London Road station, like Midland Road station on the main line, was very much on the fringe of the town, the former being almost halfway between Wellingborough town centre and Irchester, and close to the river Nene where a mill and lock were situated. Passengers heading for the north-east of England are unlikely to have travelled to Peterborough, being deterred by the almost hour-long cross-country trek that did not even connect with the East Coast Main Line. *Tommy Tomalin*

A train has been signalled and a small group of passengers await the arrival of a train to Peterborough at Irthlingborough on 11th April 1964 – perhaps they were regular passengers embarking on their last trip prior to closure. This shot was taken looking north eastwards towards Thrapston. There are remarkable similarities between this station and Wellingborough London Road which suggests this style was adopted as standard on this section of line. Note the three gables, canopies and decorative chimneys – clearly no expense was spared when the line was constructed.
Edwin Wilmshurst

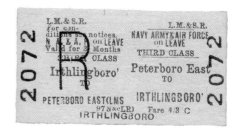

The town of Thrapston boasted passenger services on two separate routes at one time but those on the Kettering to Cambridge line via Huntingdon, which served Midland Road station, were withdrawn in June 1959, leaving only the Northampton to Peterborough line. Sadly, this suffered the same fate in May 1964, as previously mentioned, and Thrapston was left without any rail connection. In this picture Stanier Class 5MT 4-6-0 No.45301 eases into Bridge Street station with the 6.00pm stopping train from Peterborough East to Northampton on 2nd May 1962, the last westbound train on Mondays to Fridays. Like others on the line the station building had three gables and was gas lit; tubs of flowers were a particularly attractive feature. Railway aficionados would probably have been more interested in the goods yard, however, where there was a wagon turntable which enabled wagons to be pushed into the goods shed.
Tommy Tomalin

The 6.00pm from Peterborough (East) is seen again, this time on 29th July 1963, with 'Black Five' No.45050 pulling away from its Thrapston station stop on a lovely summer's evening. The farmer appears to have been very busy in the adjacent field! This picture was taken from the former Kettering to Cambridge line where it passed over the Northampton line just south of Thrapston (Bridge Street) station. This shot vividly illustrates the reason for the route's demise: three coaches suffice for the meagre amount of passenger traffic on offer. The last eastbound train, the 6.39pm Northampton (Castle) to Peterborough (East) on 2nd May 1964, was headed by Stanier Class 5MT No.45113, suitably decorated with a laurel wreath. This last working was packed to the gunwales with local people, and a large contingent of enthusiasts, making a melancholy last

return trip and the platforms at many intermediate stations were crowded with 'last day' mourners. On arrival at Peterborough the wreath was transferred to another Stanier Class 5MT, No.44837, and this had the dubious privilege of powering the very last regular passenger train. Oundle station was thronged with people, while at Barnwell, where somebody had rigged up a powerful floodlight, the platforms were draped with black flags and an impromptu fireworks display was staged which, hopefully, lifted the gloomy atmosphere for a time. Later, the final train from Wellingborough arrived at Northampton behind Ivatt-designed Class 2MT 2-6-2T No.41219, coincidentally a 'veteran' of the last train to Blisworth on 2nd January 1960. *Tommy Tomalin*

This portrait of Barnwell station was taken on 25th April 1962 with two passengers waiting for an evening train to Northampton. The wooden waiting room was constructed in 1884 for the use of the royal family when they visited Barnwell Manor, the home of the Duke of Gloucester. In 1977 the structure was moved to the Nene Valley Railway where it can still be seen at the time of writing. Part of the station house is visible behind the waiting room and this is still in existence in private ownership. On 14th June 1963 the Royal Train conveyed HM the Queen to Barnwell thus maintaining the station's royal connections, but it is not known whether Her Majesty used the waiting room! Note that the nameboard is painted in dark blue indicating that the station came under the jurisdiction of the Eastern Region. *Tommy Tomalin*

Oundle station is seen in this view, looking south-westwards towards Thrapston, on 11th April 1964. Oundle station had staggered platforms with no overlap and this explains why only one platform is visible in this photograph – the other one was behind the photographer. The station house, which is depicted here, was designed in the Jacobean style by J W Livock and constructed of local stone; it survives in private ownership at the time of writing. When the station was first opened there were small goods yards on each side of the main line tracks and both had wagon turntables that were connected by a track that crossed the main line at right angles. This unusual arrangement lasted until 1926 when the yard on the up side was extended and the turntables removed. Goods traffic routed via Peterborough was handled here long after the withdrawal of regular passenger services in 1964 and school specials also continued to run to and from Oundle, these continuing until 1972. The final passenger working, a rail tour formed of a diesel unit, took place on 4th November 1972 and the line was closed completely two days later. *Edwin Wilmshurst*

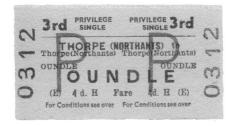

In 1836 the South Midland Railway was proposed from Leicester to Northampton with a branch to Market Harborough but nothing came immediately of this plan, however the Midland Counties Railway, which ran from Leicester to Rugby, was constructed and opened in 1840. The former scheme was revived during the Railway Mania of 1845 and this time included a branch from Market Harborough to Bedford, but the scheme lapsed due to a shortage of money, only to be revived yet again in 1851 when the financial outlook was brighter. There was considerable clamour in both towns for a direct link to London and furthermore, in 1852, the Midland Railway (MR) despatched 352,000 tons of coal to London via Rugby, which was then the only practical route available, and this increased the desirability of its own independent line. There was also the possibility of exploiting substantial iron ore deposits in Northamptonshire. In 1853 the MR shareholders approved an extension of the former Midland Counties Railway (which by this time had become part of the MR) from Leicester to Bedford and Hitchin, and various landowners along the route, who were fervent supporters of the line, offered their land at a price that reflected merely the agricultural value – a valuable concession. On 4th August 1853 the necessary Bill was approved by Parliament with little opposition but in some ways this landmark was merely the beginning of the MR's problems because, with the onset of the Crimean war, money was short and the MR's shareholders could only produce £1 million to pay for the massive construction planned. The MR's chairman, John Ellis, told the contractors, in effect, that the line would have to be built to a budget within the available finance or not at all and the result was 'a great deal of scraping' to quote one of the engineers. There was only one tunnel but three major summits with that at Sharnbrook being approached from the north by three miles of 1 in 120 gradient. The line was initially double track but was later quadrupled and gradients eased by building a deviation. The line was opened for coal traffic on 15th April 1857 and to passenger trains on 8th May, and the opening day was apparently observed as a holiday in some towns along the route with special trains being laid on for the local populace. Trains to London terminated at King's Cross from February 1858 but in 1863 the MR presented a Bill to Parliament for an extension from Bedford to London, but that is another story, as they say, outside the scope of this book. In this illustration Stanier Class 8F No.48651 is depicted at the former Irchester station with a ballast working on 15th September 1963; this shot was taken looking towards Wellingborough. Irchester station lost its passenger service from 7th March 1960 but looks remarkably neat and intact in this photograph. *Tommy Tomalin*

Stanier Class 5MT 4-6-0 No.45211 emits a volcanic smoke effect as it charges through Wellingborough (Midland Road) station with a London-bound fast freight on 11th April 1964; note the splendid platform gas lamp standard in the foreground. 1964 proved to be the last year that steam locomotives could be observed in any number on the southern section of the Midland Main Line south of Wellingborough because steam servicing facilities were withdrawn from Cricklewood shed on 13th December, from which date its last seven locomotives were transferred away. During the last few weeks prior to that date Class 8F 2-8-0s and 9F 2-10-0s continued to work a variety of goods trains but undoubtedly the highlight was the unprecedented appearance of Gresley Class A3 Pacific No.60112 *St Simon* on the 4.55am Chaddesden to St Pancras freight on 7th December. The visitor did not return, however, because the Pacific was used on the GC line before returning home to York. A morning Leeds to Bedford parcels working sometimes produced a Holbeck-based 'Jubilee' while 'Jubilee' 4-6-0 No.45626 *Seychelles* was noted on a down fitted freight on 12th December. Sporadic steam workings continued for some time afterwards, principally on coal trains to Goldington power station near Bedford. *Edwin Wilmshurst*

2nd · SINGLE   SINGLE · 2nd
1461   Wellingborough (Lon. Rd.) to   1461
Wellingborough (London Road)   Wellingborough (London Road)
Wellingborough (Midland Road)   Wellingborough (Midland Road)
WELLINGBOROUGH
(MIDLAND ROAD)
(M)   0/4   Fare   0/4   (M)
For conditions see over   For conditions see over

A scene at the north end of Wellingborough (Midland Road) station on 30th April 1964 showing Ivatt Class 2MT 2-6-2T No.41225 simmering after arrival with the 6.27pm train from Northampton (Castle); this locomotive was one of a number of the class fitted with pull-push equipment for motor working. This service was withdrawn from 4th May 1964 when the cross-country Northampton to Wellingborough/Peterborough trains ran for the last time. The 1963 summer timetable advertised a service of ten trains a day between Northampton and Wellingborough (Midland Road), some of which continued to Kettering and Leicester. The service on to Peterborough via Thrapston, consisted of only six trains on Mondays to Fridays while an extra evening service was provided on Saturdays. Neither route had any timetabled trains on Sundays. It should be noted that the Peterborough services stopped only at Wellingborough London Road station and did not serve Midland Road which was reached by a spur line to the Midland main line. *Tommy Tomalin*

A number of Class 9F 2-10-0s, Nos.92020 to 92029, were experimentally built with Crosti boilers in an effort to reduce coal consumption; the locomotives involved entered traffic in 1955. They were very distinctive machines because the chimney was only used for lighting up, the exhaust being discharged from a separate outlet along the side of the boiler near the cab. Unfortunately, the results were disappointing and, furthermore, the engines experienced problems with excessive corrosion which put paid to the experiment. In early March 1959 five Crosti-boilered locomotives were reportedly stored unserviceable at Wellingborough shed and in this picture a line of three engines can be seen with No.92021 nearest to the camera, with Nos.92023 and 92026 behind. No.92021 was overhauled at Crewe works in 1960 and its boiler converted to operate conventionally; it remained in traffic until November 1967.
W. Potter / R.C. Riley collection

On 7th March 1965 the Home Counties Railway Society ran an enthusiasts' special from London Paddington to Wellingborough via Stratford-upon-Avon and Rugby; later the train returned to London via Oxford. Titled the 'Six Counties Rail Tour' the train was powered throughout by Southern Region steam in the shape of Maunsell U Class 'Mogul' No.31639 and Bulleid Q1 Class 0-6-0 No.33006; both classes were being rapidly thinned out at the time. Here, the two visitors look somewhat out of place against the background of BR/Sulzer 'Peak' 1Co-Co1 diesels and a Stanier 'Black Five' berthed on Wellingborough shed but they were no doubt of considerable interest to local spotters, especially the Q1 Class with its most unusual design features. The history of Wellingborough shed can be traced back to 1868 when a roundhouse, later known as Engine Shed No.1, was built and a four-road fitting shop appeared in 1869. Another roundhouse, Engine Shed No.2, opened in 1872, the MR having accepted a tender of just over £10,000. In LMS days new coal and ash plants were provided, the roof of the older shed was reconditioned and a new 60ft turntable installed. Henceforth No.1 shed was generally used as the running shed while No.2 shed was used for maintenance purposes such as boiler washouts and mileage examinations. In the early 1920s the allocation comprised 80 0-6-0s that were the staple power on heavy goods work but the arrival of Fowler 0-8-0s in 1929 and the Garratts during 1930 naturally resulted in some 0-6-0s being displaced; their ranks were further depleted when 30 Stanier Class 8F 2-8-0s were allocated to the shed. In 1954 a substantial batch of BR Standard Class 9F 2-10-0s, including the ten Crosti-boilered examples, was based at Wellingborough. The No.1 shed was demolished in 1964 but the steam allocation lasted until 13th June 1966, after which date the depot survived servicing diesels. *Martin Smith*

A view of the railway installations at Wellingborough, with a huge goods shed and warehouse dominating the down side of the main line and a Class 8F simmering in the yard. On the left of the picture the buildings comprising Wellingborough shed can just be discerned. A nicely cleaned Class 4F 0-6-0, No.44414, passes by on the up fast line *en route* to Luton to work a rail tour. Organised by the South Bedfordshire Locomotive Club, the tour visited the Newport Pagnell branch and later traversed the line linking Blisworth to Wellingborough via Northampton Bridge Street, a route that has since been erased from the railway map. The participants were then treated to a trip along the Higham Ferrers branch, which was a goods only branch by that time, before journeying back to Luton along the Midland main line. A really interesting afternoon jaunt along lines long since consigned to history. This photograph was taken on 19th September 1964.
Graham Onley

On 30th March 1968 steam traction staged a very brief comeback on the Midland main line when BR Standard Class 4MT No.75029 and Class 9F No.92203 travelled up to Cricklewood under their own steam. Both locomotives had been purchased from BR by the world-famous artist David Shepherd and were *en route* to the Longmoor Military Railway in Hampshire; they are seen here passing Finedon Road signal box, north of Wellingborough. The locomotives' journey to Hampshire appears to have been rather protracted because they did not reach their destination until 7th April and were presumably stabled at Cricklewood in the meantime. At least they made the final stage under their own steam, quite an achievement bearing in mind steam on the Southern Region finished in July 1967. Finedon station, which closed as long ago as 2nd December 1940, was some miles to the north of Finedon Road. *Robin Patrick*

Regular steam workings on the Midland main line became fewer and fewer as 1965 progressed, the trains most likely to produce steam being coal trains to Goldington power station near Bedford, as previously mentioned. The spirits of local enthusiasts were probably lifted, however, when the legendary Gresley Pacific No.4472 *Flying Scotsman* hauled a Gainsborough Model Railway Society special along the Midland main line on 11th September 1965; it was photographed just south of Kettering. The train was apparently *en route* to Kensington (Olympia) and had doubtless originated in Lincolnshire. The participants presumably returned home behind diesel traction because it was the start of a very busy weekend for No.4472 which powered a London to Weymouth tour the following day; the tour started at Waterloo but returned to Paddington via Yeovil.
Tommy Tomalin

An everyday scene at Kettering as BR Standard Class 9F 2-10-0 No.92123 passes through the station with a coal train on 17th August 1957. This locomotive was one of 36 Class 9Fs allocated to Wellingborough shed at the time for working heavy coal trains along the Midland main line and further locomotives of this class were based at Leicester shed, so this gives some indication of their important role in moving this traffic. Note the gentleman holding a child in his arms while a young lad admires the 9F as it passes the station – both youngsters were no doubt budding train spotters. Kettering station is renowned for its exceptionally decorative station canopies, some of which are just visible. *RCTS photo archive*

The old order on the Midland main line. An unidentified southbound express approaches Kettering station on 30th May 1959 behind Class 2P 4-4-0 No.40504 piloting Stanier Class 5MT No.44861. Kettering North signal box can be seen on the right of the shot while the motive power depot is immediately behind the photographer. In 1959 the diesel invasion of the route had barely started, apart from some outer suburban multiple units at the London end, and Midland Compound Class 4P and 2P 4-4-0s could still be seen at St Pancras, though their days were numbered; four different examples of the former class were observed in January. On 21st April 1959 the 6.33pm St Pancras to Derby (Midland) was hauled by BR Standard Class 5MT No.73010 piloted by Class 2P No.40504 but the Class 5MT ran hot at Kettering and had to be replaced. The train eventually left there with the Class 2P as train engine piloted by Class 9F No.92125. On other occasions at about the same time 4-4-0s could often be seen piloting 'Britannia' Pacifics so clearly the 2Ps (especially No.40504!) were playing a vital role on the Midland main line at that time. *R.C. Riley*

A rare sight indeed – an absolutely immaculate freight locomotive! In this illustration converted Crosti- boilered 2-10-0 No.92029 poses at Kettering shed on 25th August 1962 following release from Crewe works after overhaul. This machine was modified for conventional operation in 1960 and lasted in service until November 1967. It was one of a total of seven Crosti-boilered locomotives withdrawn from traffic during that month.
Tommy Tomalin

A section of the Midland main line retained semaphore signalling well into the 1980s and was often referred to as the 'Leicester gap' due to its location between two long-established stretches of colour light signalling. This absolutely delightful example of Midland Railway signalling practice could be admired at Desborough & Rothwell station and was just the kind of thing that made the study of railways such an enjoyable hobby; presumably it survived until this stretch of line was re-signalled. What a gem! This picture was taken on 23rd June 1962. *Tommy Tomalin*

Railway photography can be very frustrating, and sometimes photographers who have been waiting for some time to take a particular picture can be left fuming when a train on an adjacent line comes along at the wrong moment. In this case luck was on the photographer's side, and the 8.05am St Pancras to Manchester (Central) can be seen speeding to its next station stop at Leicester while 8F Class 2-8-0 No.48644 plods along on the up line with a coal train. An industrial branch to a local ironstone quarry can be seen on the right. *Tommy Tomalin*

Photographed against the background of the massive steel plant, Stanier Class 8F 2-8-0 No.48530, in charge of (what appears to be) a ballast train, waits in the yard at Corby on 11th May 1964; however an impudent works shunter on the adjacent track emits a volcanic exhaust and steals the show. What a cheek! The giant Stewarts & Lloyds works, which specialised in manufacturing tubes, was developed in the 1930s and was in full production by 1937, and in the early 1970s 450,000 tons of tubes were produced annually. Most of the raw materials, such as coal and limestone, was brought in by rail and the end product was despatched by the same means, so the whole operation produced considerable revenue for BR. On 18th April 1966 Corby became one of the largest towns in England to lose its passenger trains but a token service was

later re-instated in BR days, despite the fact that Corby new town was developed away from the railway and buses no doubt catered for local traffic. At the time of writing Corby enjoys a regular through service to London and there are even a few trains northwards to the neighbouring towns of Oakham and Melton Mowbray – what a turnaround. The first goods trains ran on the Glendon (just north of Kettering) to Nottingham line on 1st November 1879 and local passenger workings commenced from 2nd February 1880. Through services from London St Pancras to Nottingham and beyond followed on 1st June 1880. *R.C. Riley*

The Glendon to Nottingham line features heavy earthworks, including nine tunnels, and Harringworth viaduct which takes the line over the river Welland. The approaches to Corby involve moderate climbs in each direction and in this illustration Stanier Class 8F No.48267, working a heavy freight train, appears to be labouring as it comes up the 1 in 200 climb from Gretton station on 6th November 1965. The train is about to plunge into the 1,926yds-long Corby tunnel and the passage of this bore was no doubt a most unpleasant experience for the footplate crew, particularly bearing in mind the exhaust fumes being produced by the Class 8F. *Tommy Tomalin*

Another Class 8F, No.48317, hauling an enormously long train of mineral wagons, is seen toiling up the gradient towards Corby tunnel on the same day. The river Welland is lost somewhere in the distant landscape; the river forms part of the county border with Rutland which is about 1½ miles from the line. Like Corby the wayside station of Gretton, which served the village of that name, was closed in April 1966. *Tommy Tomalin*

BR Standard Class 9F 2-10-0 No.92083, from Wellingborough shed, creates a magnificent smokescreen as it pounds through the former Harringworth station with a long southbound coal train on 24th April 1957. The train has just passed over the impressive Harringworth viaduct. This magnificent structure, constructed in red and blue brick, is 1,275 yards-long and consists of no fewer than 82 arches with a 40ft span; the maximum height from the valley floor is 60ft. Fine views of the surrounding countryside can be obtained from trains crossing the viaduct and, in times gone by, Seaton station, on the Rugby to Peterborough line, could be clearly seen a little to the south-west. Interestingly, southbound workings enter the viaduct on a falling gradient but this changes to a 1 in 200 rising gradient which no doubt accounts for No.92083's fine display in this picture. *RCTS Photo Archive*

In the early part of the 19th century the small town of Higham Ferrers was effectively in the hands of the Duchy of Lancaster which restricted building, and its population growth was less than the neighbouring town of Rushden where development was not restrained. When the Wellingborough to Peterborough line opened in 1845 both towns were served by 'Higham Ferrers' station (later Irthlingborough) from where horse buses plied into the towns. Despite the fact that Rushden's shoe trade was expanding the towns did not appear on the railway map until much later. In 1890 a new line was authorised from Irchester Junction, just south of Wellingborough, to Raunds where a connection with the Kettering to Huntingdon line was envisaged. In the event a landowner at Raunds refused to sell his land and consequently the line managed to get no further than Higham Ferrers, just 4¾ miles from Wellingborough, which considerably restricted its usefulness; the opening date for passenger trains was 1st May 1894. The initial service of six trains each way had increased to ten by 1901 and by the 1950s there were around twelve weekday trains in each direction, but none on Sundays. Like so many lines in Northamptonshire passenger traffic was easy prey to regular bus services, especially so on this line because Wellingborough station is somewhat remote from the town centre, and the last passenger trains ran on 13th June 1959; exceptions were special seaside trains during the towns' holiday fortnight. The line remained open for regular goods traffic, however, until 1969 when it shut completely. In this portrait Fowler 2-6-4T No.42350 pauses at Rushden station with the 'Fernie' rail tour on 25th August 1962 while soberly dressed enthusiasts chat on the platform or, in some cases, walk along the track beside the locomotive. One wonders how today's Health & Safety officials would react to such irresponsible behaviour! *Tommy Tomalin*

Predictably, perhaps, railway photographers did not flock to photograph trains on the Higham Ferrers branch and only two pictures of trains on the line were submitted for inclusion in this book and, equally predictably, both depict the 'Fernie' rail tour. Here, No.42350 awaits departure from Higham Ferrers where participants were astonished to find that the station still retained a stock of printed tickets despite being open for holiday trains on only a couple of days per year! Note that Higham Ferrers was constructed as a through station with the projected extension to Raunds in mind. This rail tour must have been a really relaxing and enjoyable ramble over lines that have largely long since disappeared from the railway map. During the course of the day participants were treated to a trip over the Northampton to Market Harborough route, the Uppingham branch, plus the Seaton to Peterborough and Bedford to Northampton lines. They even managed to fit in a jaunt along the stub of the Kettering to Huntingdon branch as far as Thrapston and to ensure everybody was well fed a buffet car was included in the formation. What more could one wish for? *Tommy Tomalin*

The neat and tidy station building at Higham Ferrers is seen in this portrait which was taken on 25th April 1959, less than two months before closure to regular passenger workings. One of the posters exhorts people to 'travel by train' to Leicester while the platform seats have the station's name embossed upon them, just as well because there is no station nameboard or other sign visible. *Ron Gammage*

Extract from London Midland Region summer 1959 timetable

Table **199**—

WELLINGBOROUGH AND HIGHAM FERRERS

WEEKDAYS ONLY   SECOND CLASS ONLY

Miles			a.m.	a.m.	SX a.m.	SO a.m.	a.m.	SO a.m.	a.m.	p.m.	p.m.	SO p.m.	SX p.m.	SO p.m.	p.m.	p.m.	p.m.	p.m.	p.m.
61	NORTHAMPTON Castle . . . dep.	.	.	7 08	7 8	7	.	.	10 13	11 46	2 40	2 40	.	.	4 24	4 24	.	6 27	.	8 57	.
180	LEICESTER London Road . . . . "	. . .	. . .	7 42	7 50	8 B55	9 50	11 D18	1	7	12H50	.	3 20	3 21	5 20	5 20	6F34	. . .	8 45
180	LONDON St. Pancras . . . . "	4 20	.	.	8 15	9 20	11 15	1	5	.	.	3 20	4 55	5 30	.	6 55	8 15
0	WELLINGBOROUGH Mid. Rd. .dep.	6 35	7 50	8 36	8 46	10	5	11 25	1p 0	3	10	3 52	4 35	5	5 55	20	6 347	10 8	10 9	23	10 0
3½	Rushden	6A 52	8	1	8 44	8 54	10 C19	11 33	1G 14	3	19	4	0	4 46	5 16	5 31	6 42	7 20	8 20	9 31	10 10
4¼	HIGHAM FERRERS . . . . arr.	6 55	8	5	8 48	8 58	10 22	11 37	1	17	3 23	4	44	50	5 20	5 35	6 46	7 24	8 24	9 35	10 14

A—Arrives Rushden 6.43 a.m.   B—Depart Leicester London Road 8.57 a.m. on Saturdays.   C—Arrives Rushden 10.13 a.m.
D—Departs Leicester London Road 10.22 a.m. on Saturdays.   F—Departs Leicester London Road 6.40 p.m. on Saturdays.
G—Arrives Rushden 1.8 p.m.   H—Departs Leicester London Road 1.7 p.m. on Saturdays.   **SO**—Saturdays only.   **SX**—Saturdays excepted.
p—p.m.

Miles			a.m.	a.m.	SX a.m.	SO a.m.	a.m.	SO am	p.m.	p.m.	SO p.m.	p.m.	SO p.m.	SX p.m.	SO p.m.	p.m.	p.m.	p.m.	p.m.
0	HIGHAM FERRERS . . . . dep.	7	0	8 10	8 52	9	2	10 30	11A57	1 25	3 28	4 10	4 55	5 25	5 45	6 50	7 30	8 33	9 40	10 20
1	Rushden	7	3	8 13	8 55	9	5	10 33	12 0	1 28	3 31	4 13	4 58	5 28	5 48	6 53	7 33	8 36	9 43	10 23
4¼	WELLINGBOROUGH Mid. Rd. ... arr.	7	10	8 20	9	2	9	12	10 40	12 10	1 35	3 38	4 20	5	5	35	5 55	7	0	7 40	8 43	9 50	10 30
69½	180 LONDON St. Pancras . . . . . arr.	9	11	9F 50	11	7	10 52	12G40	.	3C18	.	5J55	.	7 47	7 47	.	9H14	10 55	.
38½	180 LEICESTER London Road . . . . "	8 48	9K 44	9 44	10	1	11 44	1 22	3E23	6	6	6 66	17	7 38	7 40	7 57	. . .	10	0	10 50	11 29
18	61 NORTHAMPTON Castle . . . . . . "	8	19L 11	.	.	11 36	.	2D24	4	5	.	6 15	6 15	.	7SX43	8B47	.	10 24	.

A—Through train to Leicester London Rd. (Table 180).   H—Arrive London St. Pancras 9.56 p.m. on Saturdays.
B—Arrive Northampton Castle 8.39 p.m. on Saturdays.   J—Arrive London St. Pancras 6.10 p.m. on Saturdays.
C—Arrive London St. Pancras 3.28 p.m. on Saturdays.   K—Arrive Leicester London Road 10.1 a.m. on Saturdays.
D—Arrive Northampton Castle 2.34 p.m. on Saturdays.   L—Arrive Northampton Castle 9.12 a.m. on Saturdays.
E—Arrive Leicester London Road 3.20 p.m. on Saturdays.   **SO**—Saturdays only.
F—Arrive London St. Pancras 10.16 a.m. on Saturdays.   **SX**—Saturdays excepted.
G—Arrive London St. Pancras 1.7 p.m. on Saturdays.

Looking for all the world as if it had just been taken out of a gigantic packing case, this is how the newly reconstructed station at Banbury looked on 4th July 1959 – the only blemish being the smoke marks on the footbridge. The main building at ground level was built using a reinforced concrete frame and houses the booking office while a spacious concourse provides access to a bookstall, public telephones and other facilities. The 40ft-wide covered bridge includes waiting and refreshment rooms, both of which provide a commanding view of approaching trains; there is also a separate passageway for the transfer of luggage and mails between the platforms. The station is centrally heated and lit by fluorescent lamps and BR publicity at the time claimed that cleanliness, light and fresh air were the station's hallmarks – and who would argue with that? When the premises were rebuilt the opportunity was taken to modify the track layout at Banbury that had been such a bottleneck and a new down relief loop line was laid; various long-standing speed restrictions were also eased. The station may have been new but there are many reminders in this shot (apart from the steam engine!) that the modernisation of BR was still in its infancy at this time: note the semaphore signals, water crane, slip coach on the right and stock of a Woodford Halse 'local' in the bay platform. *John Langford*

Closed to passenger traffic from New Year's Day 1968, few routes have such a chequered history as the Oxford to Bletchley line, part of which has recently become a new route for through services between London and Oxford. The Oxford & Bletchley Railway opened on 20th May 1851 and eventually became a section of the 77 miles-long cross country line stretching from Oxford to Bedford and Cambridge. In the 1959 summer timetable seven weekday trains were advertised between Oxford and Bletchley but it should be noted that these were supplemented east of Verney Junction by additional workings to and from Buckingham and Banbury. The 1955 BR Modernisation Plan included a call for development of the line as a freight link between the east coast ports and south Wales, and an expensive flyover was constructed at Bletchley to avoid conflicting moves with the WCML. The plan coincided with a rapid downturn in BR freight carryings and was soon abandoned but not before land was purchased at Swanbourne for a huge mechanised marshalling yard. What a gigantic white elephant that would have been! In late 1963 BR had a total reversal of policy and proposed the closure of the entire Oxford to Cambridge route which was one of the most controversial proposals of the Beeching era. Local people were particularly incensed as only the local stations, and not the entire service, were recommended for closure in the Beeching Report. Despite considerable opposition all passenger trains on the Oxford to Bletchley section ceased on 1st January 1968, as previously stated. In this picture Fowler-designed Class 4MT 2-6-4T No.42368 is seen at Swanbourne with the 5.05pm Bletchley to Oxford train on 4th July 1959.
John Langford

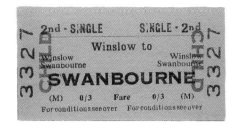

Railway photographers have often taken a gamble to obtain an exceptional shot and here the photographer appears to be risking a drenching as Stanier Class 5MT No.45314, powering a southbound holiday special, picks up water from Castlethorpe troughs on 5th August 1962. The weather appears to be fine, with lovely puffy clouds marching across the sky, so perhaps he dried-off quickly in the sunshine! In early 1965 the LMR announced what was tantamount to a 'closure programme' for the various sets of water troughs on the Western Division and those on the fast lines at Castlethorpe were due to be withdrawn from 14th March. The troughs on the slow lines, which were doubtless much more likely to be used by steam traction, lasted until 26th September from which date yet another spectacle of the steam age at Castlethorpe was consigned to history. Stand clear of the overflow! *Tommy Tomalin*

There were two schemes for new routes in the 1840s that would have provided Newport Pagnell with a train service but both fell by the wayside. One of those envisaged a line from Bletchley to Wellingborough via Newport Pagnell and Olney and this was revived in 1863, but the projection beyond Newport Pagnell was subsequently abandoned. The townspeople must have wondered if they would ever have the benefit of a railway service but on 2nd September 1867 a short, 4 miles-long branch from Wolverton was opened. Prior to the First World War the line carried around a dozen weekday trains in each direction, but by the late 1950s this figure had shrunk to around six each way. The long building on the horizon in this illustration is part of Wolverton carriage works which was opened by the LBR in 1838, the location apparently being selected because Wolverton was midway between London and Birmingham. The works was the chief repair depot for both locomotives and carriages until 1861 when all locomotive work was transferred to Crewe and henceforth it concentrated on carriage building and overhauls. The works was at its peak in 1900, employing 5,000 men and covering 35 acres. In this rare colour photograph of a timetabled steam passenger train on the Newport Pagnell branch, Ivatt Class 2MT 2-6-2T No.41222 is seen heading the 10.00am train from Wolverton on 22nd September 1962. The placid stretch of water on the right is the Grand Union canal. *Tommy Tomalin*

The Northampton to Bedford line was promoted by a local company and opened on 10th June 1872; it was worked by the MR from the outset and that Company acquired the line in 1885. Originally it was proposed to link Bedford to Northampton and Weedon but there were considerable difficulties siting a junction at Weedon and the projection beyond Northampton was dropped. The promoting company obviously wanted to make an impact in Northampton and constructed its own station in the grounds of St John's hospital, building Guildhall Road as access. The line had an unremarkable career until the late 1950s when four-wheel diesel railbuses were introduced in an effort to cut costs and save the branch from closure. They proved a mixed blessing, however, due to their propensity to slip on frosty rails, and in January 1959 steam traction returned in force as a result of the railbuses' fallibilities, but delays occurred due to the lack of auto-fitted locomotives and the need to run-round at each end of the journey. The line hit the headlines for all the wrong reasons when, on 17th June 1960, Stanier Class 8F No.48616 was damaged beyond economic repair when it was involved in a collision near Turvey; the unfortunate locomotive subsequently became the first 8F to be condemned from BR service. Rumours of closure of the line began to circulate about this time and no doubt BR's apparent failure to maintain a reliable service had alienated many regular customers. The last passenger trains operated on Saturday 3rd March 1962 and here, on an appropriately miserable day, the 11.40am from Bedford to Northampton, propelled by an unidentified Ivatt Class 2MT 2-6-2T, is seen entering Olney station. The route was closed to all through traffic in January 1964 and subsequently Oakley Junction, where it joined the St Pancras to Leicester main line, was taken out in mid-1965. *Tommy Tomalin*

Extract from London Midland Region summer 1959 timetable

Table 197—	BEDFORD AND NORTHAMPTON	WEEKDAYS ONLY	SECOND CLASS ONLY																
Miles		a.m.		SX a.m.	SO a.m.	E SO a.m.	SX p.m.	SO p.m.	p.m.	SX p.m.	p.m.	p.m.		p.m.					
—	195 LONDON St. Pancras ... dep	4 20	...	5 55	8 15	9 20	11a15	11a15	...	12 55	3 20	5 30	...	6 55	...	...	...		
0	BEDFORD Midland Road ... dep	6 40	.	8 10	9 49	11 30	12 40	1 17	1 40	3 18	4 50	6 53	.	8 30	.	.	...		
6	Turvey	6 50	.	8 24	9 59	11 40	12 52	1 27	1 50	3 28	5 07	3	...	8 40	...	...	...		
10¼	Olney	6 58		8 32	10 7	11 48	1 0	1 35	1 58	3 36	5 8	7 11	...	8 48	...	...	...		
15½	Piddington	...			10 15	11 56	1 11	1 43	2 6	3 44					...	...	...		
21	NORTHAMPTON Bridge Street ... arr	7 13		8 48	10 24	12 5	1 22	1 52	2 15	3 53	5 23	7 26	...	9 3	...	...	...		
22¼	" Castle ... arr	7 17		8 51	10 27	12 8	1 26	1 59	2 18	3 56	5 27	7 30	...	9 9	...	...	...		

Miles		SX a.m.	SO a.m.	SX a.m.	SO a.m.	SX a.m.	p.m.	SX p.m.	SO p.m.	SX p.m.	p.m.	p.m.		p.m.				
0	NORTHAMPTON Castle ... dep	7 56	7 56	9 5	10 25	10 38	12 12	2 10	3 8	4 2	6 7	7 40	...	9 18	...	...	...	
1	" Bridge Street ...	7 58	7 58	9 7	10 27	10 40	12 14	2 12	3 12	4 4	6 9	7 42	.	9 20	.	.	...	
7¼	Piddington	...		9 16	10 36	10 49	12 23	2 21	3 21						...	...	...	
12	Olney	8 14	8 14	9 24	10 44	10 57	12 31	2 29	3 29	4 20	6 25	7 58	.	9 36	.	.	...	
16½	Turvey	8 24	8 24	9 32	10 52	11 5	12 39	2 37	3 37	4 28	6 33	8 6	.	9 44	.	.	...	
22½	BEDFORD Midland Road ... arr	8 38	8 35	9 43	11 3	11 16	12 50	2 48	3 48	4 44	6 44	8 17		9 55	...	...	...	
72¼	195 LONDON St. Pancras ... arr	9 50	10 2	11 7	1p 7	12p40	3B 8	4 30	5 30	5 55	9C20	9 D44		11 55	...	...	...	

B—Arrive London (St. Pancras) 2.52 p.m. on Saturdays.
C—Arrive London (St. Pancras) 9.27 p.m. on Fridays, 8.53 p.m. on Saturdays.
D—Arrives London (St. Pancras) 9.56 p.m. on Saturdays.
E—Conveys First and Second Class passengers.
SO—Saturdays only.   SX—Saturdays excepted.
a—a.m.
p—p.m.

Mention the name 'Seaton' to most people and they will immediately think of the well-known holiday resort in Devon. But this picture was taken at the other Seaton, in Rutland, whose modest junction station served a small village. The first route through Seaton to be opened was a line from Rugby to Luffenham (near Stamford) which was brought into use throughout on 2nd June 1851, while the line to Peterborough (East), which later became the busier route, dated from 1st November 1879. In this view of Seaton station taken on 23rd May 1959 London Tilbury & Southend Railway (LTSR)-designed Class 3P 4-4-2T No.41975 'blows off' prior to departure with the 11.10am to Uppingham. This 3¾ miles-long branch was a latecomer on the railway map, not opening until 1st October 1894; this late 'appearance' was due to the fact that Uppingham was well served by nearby Manton station. The last regular passenger trains ran on 11th June 1960 but schools specials and goods traffic lasted until 30th May 1964. Passenger services on the Luffenham and Peterborough routes were withdrawn from 6th June 1966 from which date Seaton station closed. *David Soggee*

The 50¾ miles-long Rugby to Peterborough line served few intermediate centres of population, the only exception being Market Harborough, and this picture of the empty countryside around Seaton station was, apparently, fairly representative of the route. Seaton was just the kind of station that was a joy to railway enthusiasts where nothing happened for hours and then, suddenly, trains appeared from all directions. Here, a four-coach Rugby to Peterborough (East) working has just arrived and makes connections with trains to Stamford and Uppingham that are waiting patiently in the bay platform. This burst of activity, however, does not seem to have produced many passengers which hardly augurs well for the route's future. Note the three-way junction signal at the platform end and also the fact that the LTSR-designed tank engines had been ousted by Ivatt 2-6-2Ts by this date. One of the arches of nearby Harringworth viaduct is just visible on the right. *David Soggee*

The 12.24pm train to Seaton awaits departure from Uppingham station on 23rd May 1959 – note the brake van which indicates it was booked to run as a 'mixed' train conveying both passenger and goods traffic. Judging by the woebegone condition of its paintwork the local station painting gang seemed to have overlooked Uppingham which doesn't appear to have been touched since nationalisation! An old LMSR 'hawkseye' station nameboard is prominent in the foreground. The train engine is LTSR-designed 4-4-2T No.41975: a trio of these delightful 4-4-2Ts was allocated to Spital Bridge shed, Peterborough, for duties on the Uppingham and Stamford branches from Seaton. When the Uppingham branch closed Ivatt 2-6-2Ts supplied by Market Harborough shed continued to work the Stamford trains which eventually became the last 'pull-push' operation on BR, lasting until diesel units took over on 4th October 1965. *David Soggee*

A train to Seaton, with former LTSR Class 3P 4-4-2T No.41975 in charge, is depicted at Stamford (Town) station on 31st May 1958. There were two stations in the town originally, the other one, Stamford (East), being served by branch trains to and from Essendine on the East Coast Main Line. The latter station was closed on 4th March 1957 when services were diverted to Stamford (Town) but this arrangement lasted only a couple of years, the branch being closed completely from 15th June 1959. Stamford (Town) station is a gem and an attractive gateway to the delightful town it serves which is just over the Northamptonshire county border in Lincolnshire. No.41975 was constructed at Derby to the original LTSR design, entered traffic in February 1930 and lasted until withdrawn in November 1959, when it was probably the last operational survivor. Ivatt Class 2MT 2-6-2Ts took over the Seaton workings until the line came under the axe, as previously stated, on 6th June 1966. *R.C. Riley*

Trains approaching Stamford from the east pass through a deep cutting, and under a succession of bridges before entering the station and these are visible in the background of this illustration of Stanier Class 4MT 2-6-4T No.42541 arriving on 25th June 1960. The precise identity of the train is unknown but at the time of the photograph No.42541 was allocated to Rugby shed so it is logical to assume it was a Peterborough to Rugby train via Market Harborough. This was another cross-country line that, at first glance, looked a valuable route on paper but in reality served no significant settlements not served by other railway lines. The 1959 summer timetable lists nine weekday trains, supplemented on Saturdays by seasonal holiday workings which did not materially contribute to the service. Stopping trains took a leisurely 1½ hours to cover the 50¾ miles between Rugby and Peterborough where they arrived at the East station rather than Peterborough (North) which would have been more convenient for most long distance travellers. *Ron Gammage*

A lady and two young boys are captivated as Ivatt Class 2MT 2-6-0 No.46445 rolls into Countesthorpe station with the 4.58pm SO Leicester to Rugby train on 22nd July 1961. This unexciting branch latterly had a very meagre service of around half a dozen trains in each direction on weekdays only, and the onlookers seen here were probably unaware that many years previously it was part of a major trunk route from the east Midlands to London. Backed by the coal barons who sought to transport their fuel to London, the line's history can be traced back to 1836 when the Midland Counties Railway was incorporated to build a line from Nottingham and Derby to Leicester and on to Rugby. The latter section was opened on 30th June 1840, so it was one of Great Britain's earliest routes and gave mining interests a direct line to London via the LBR. It would be an understatement, however, to say its fortunes declined when the MR opened its own route to the capital in 1868 and the Leicester to Rugby branch became a sleepy backwater. The line was closed some time before the infamous Doctor Beeching started to wield his axe, closing from 1st January 1962. *Tommy Tomalin*

There have been a number of lines where vintage motive power has been retained due to the physical limitations of the route, a classic example being the use of three Adams 'Radial' tank locomotives on the tightly-curved Lyme Regis branch long after the rest of the class had been withdrawn. Another line where restrictions applied was the branch from Desford to Leicester West Bridge upon which aged Class 2F 0-6-0s built in the 1870s lasted well into the 1960s. This line was formerly part of the Leicester & Swannington Railway (LSR), one of the earliest in Great Britain, opened on 17th July 1832, but the route was partially replaced in 1849 by a new line between Leicester and Burton-on-Trent. The LSR was constructed to convey coal from the west Leicestershire coalfield into the city of Leicester, whence it would be conveyed to other important towns by canal; its opening had a profound effect on the city's prosperity, the price of coal being reduced by 10 shillings (50p.) a ton. Passenger services were provided from the outset but the accommodation was solely on mixed trains until 1887 and most passengers no doubt preferred to use alternative services that ran to the more centrally situated Leicester (London Road) station. Passenger traffic ebbed away and the inevitable came on Saturday 22nd September 1928 when the last passenger train, the 5.30pm from West Bridge station to Desford departed, apparently packed to the gunwales, with third class travellers reportedly travelling in superior accommodation. The goods traffic was unaffected, however, and the venerable Johnson-designed Class 2Fs held sway due to the very restricted bore of the 1,796 yards-long Glenfield tunnel. By the early 1960s, however, the locomotives were showing their age and BR Standard Class 2MT 2-6-0s with cut down cab roofs ousted the Class 2Fs. The last members of the once sizeable fleet of Class 2F locomotives, Nos.58143/48/82, were based at Coalville shed and No.58148 was the last example in service, working the 5.48am Desford to West Bridge goods and 12.15pm return on 14th December 1963. No.58148, built by Beyer Peacock, entered service as long ago as March 1876 so it had certainly earned its keep. Here that machine is ambling along with a train bound for Desford on 1st August 1963. This old timer was pensioned off a few months later, truly the end of an era. *Martin Smith*

Before the advent of cheap continental holidays the vast majority of British families took their annual break by the seaside, mostly in either July or August when the schoolchildren were on holiday. In the 1950s and early 1960s car ownership was the exception rather than the rule and vast numbers of holiday-makers relied on the railway to get them to their destination, whether it was Scarborough or Sidmouth. Most hotels and guest houses worked on the basis of a weekly or fortnightly stay, usually commencing on a Saturday, and this placed enormous demands on the railway's resources. During the Beeching era this type of purely seasonal traffic, for which special sets of coaches were retained for the summer peak periods, was quickly identified as being totally uneconomic and many 'dated' holiday workings soon disappeared from the timetables. Rolling stock for the wide variety of seasonal workings was very often provided on the basis of a set of coaching stock working to a resort on one Saturday and returning the following Saturday, alternating with a set provided by another region, so the carriages were idle for long periods. This resulted in some quite exceptional workings and here nicely cleaned BR Standard 'Britannia' Pacific No.70020 *Mercury* is depicted heading a Birmingham (New Street) to Hastings holiday train near Hillmorton, just south of Rugby, on 24th August 1963. The combination of a 'Britannia' and Southern Region green-liveried stock, including both Bulleid and Maunsell-designed vehicles, was really unusual and must have been a talking point among train spotters along the WCML. A Southern Region locomotive would have replaced *Mercury* at Willesden for the rest of the journey to the south coast.
Neville Simms